Endearing Pain

for Michelle

God is good.

ever onward...

Colleen

Some things can never be put back together . . . but the pieces remain.

Endearing Pain

Life Lessons from MS Afflictions

Colleen Peters

Foreword by
Todd Sellick

RESOURCE *Publications* · Eugene, Oregon

ENDEARING PAIN
Life Lessons from MS Afflictions

Resource Publications
An Imprint of Wipf and Stock Publishers
199 W. 8th Ave., Suite 3
Eugene, OR 97401

www.wipfandstock.com

PAPERBACK ISBN: 978-1-4982-3789-5
HARDCOVER ISBN: 978-1-4982-3791-8

Manufactured in the U.S.A.   2/23/2016

For those who know no purpose in their pain.

Contents

Foreword

WHAT DOES IT MEAN to suffer, except to perhaps come to the end of ourselves, or toward the end of ourselves. And maybe when we come to this spare and sometimes unspeakably lonely place, a new conversation, and a new journey begins. A death before a new life.

When feeling competent and strong with self-sufficiency, confidence and enthusiasm, we are full of great ideas for ourselves and others. We see things so clearly, we're quite sure about our notions and methods, and that we know the way. Things we'd love to share and maybe to teach others. This mastery has its own thrill and excitement.

But when nearly everything is pulled out from beneath us, this certainty and the buoyancy and lightness that goes with it may dissolve in seconds, or more slowly over months or years.

Within a city block or two right now, there are many, young and old, grieving loss, living with sickness and in pain, anxious with fear, and with an aloneness and angst that is beyond words.

What can we begin to say to this? What can we do? Perhaps this is you right now.

In my work I meet with a handful of people each week who are wandering about in this frightening cul-de-sac. Suffering and the hopelessness that can accompany loss arrive in so many different ways in our lives, and each experience can come with a nearly unbearable and sometimes crushing weight of fear and loneliness. We know that hope is essential to life, but it can feel so quickly and so completely pulled out of our grasp. And then what?

In this book, my long-time and dear friend Colleen invites you to consider what she began to discover when her health and power began to leave her. My zaniest and liveliest of friends began to stumble, and then to fall, both figuratively and literally.

Colleen's life has taken a very different path than expected. A road not romanticized here, but rather, a tough and honest recollecting, with practical and thoughtful observations. With her illness and a thousand limitations and losses, Colleen set off on a voyage, writing to us from time to time in these letters along her way; a travelogue.

In *Endearing Pain* Colleen hasn't thought to indulge too much in the story of her particular life, perhaps having it clearly in mind that others have their own stories and lives to refer to. Instead, she has allowed her particular river of pain and loss to move her downstream at a pace not her own, but nevertheless showing her good and hopeful and even marvellous things along the canyon walls of her sometimes quiet and difficult days, always aware that God is directing the journey.

Through anxiety, uncertainly, loss and pain Colleen has experienced a kind of joy, and a life larger and more compelling and wonderful than we might imagine.

As you read, I hope you will be heartened and warmed, and challenged and encouraged. Colleen is a very good traveling companion.

Dr. Todd Sellick

Acknowledgements

I AM GRATEFUL TO Len, Nicholas, Jackson, Renée and Victoria for their great forbearance with me as I grappled with the challenges of writing a book, and to the friends who spurred me on to its completion. A special thank you to Victoria for her drawing that appears on the frontispiece and to Jan Sellick for relieving me of the arduous task of formatting the bibliography.

Abbreviations

Hebrew Bible / Old Testament

Genesis—Gen
Samuel—Sam
Job—Job
Psalms—Ps (pl. Pss)
Proverbs—Prov
Ecclesiastes—Eccl

New Testament

Mark—Mark
Luke—Luke
John—John
Romans—Rom
Corinthians—Cor
Philippians—Phil
Hebrews—Heb
John—John
Revelation—Rev

Introduction

"He who began a good work in you will perfect it until the day of Christ Jesus."

—Phil 1:6

SINCE 2004, I HAVE lived with a rare and progressive form of Multiple Sclerosis (MS) and have long struggled with giving an adequate answer when people ask me how I'm doing. That question has always been difficult for me because there are many facets to the answer. Several years ago, to alleviate my frustration with giving an inadequate short answer to the question, I tried to explain in a letter what it was like to be in my skin and how my illness affected us as a family. I have continued to write letters several times a year, all of which collectively form the backbone of this book.

In my fifty-seven years, God has approached me countless times and in countless ways, to perfect in me the good work he began when he showed me Christ and the cross. Of course, he always allows me to respond as I choose, and my responses have varied. I have ignored, shunned and on occasion embraced his invitations. Despite how I respond, God persists in love to pursue me, and will do this, I know, as long as I live. In 2004, God took unprecedented initiative with me, and this book tells the story of how God got my attention, how I reacted, and how life has unfolded in the years that ensued.

Just days before Christmas, I underwent brain surgery as doctors tried to diagnose a 'foreign body' in my brain. I had good reason to fear it would be my last Christmas with my husband Len and our kids. The fear was ferocious as days of waiting for biopsy results stretched into weeks, yet beneath it all was a peculiar peace that quelled the fear—an assurance that all would be well, come what may.

Though at the time I sensed no purpose in the waiting, I've come to appreciate those dark fear-filled days as an expression of God's loving purposes for me—a time when my tired faith was validated and then infused with a fresh vitality. Deep inside I knew, beyond a doubt, that God was in control of my chaos and that I was loved.

I was spared the diagnosis of a brain tumor and the waiting finally came to end in mid February when I got news there was no malignancy and it appeared that some sort of demyelinating disease was to blame. Given the rare type of lesions found in my brain, the definitive diagnosis of MS was still 18 months away and the labeling of the specific type of MS I have (progressive relapsing) and accompanying therapy options were many more months in coming. But as God rescued me from crisis fear in 2004, so too he has been equally gracious with the chronic fears I've faced since then, as I learn to live with a disease marked by progressive deterioration that has brought much change into my life. Though the changes have been challenging and difficult in many ways, they have also been channels of God's grace. I live with the draining reality of a chronic illness, but I live too in a Kingdom reality that renews me, and that has made all the difference. It has given me hope that fashions faith from fear and helps me see God speaking through the daily unfolding of events. My illness has certainly served to broaden my awareness of God, which in turn has deepened my understanding and appreciation of a loving sovereign God.

It's hard to say exactly how the events of 2004 affected me, but I do know that God mercifully met me at crucial times and in creative ways, and so impressed his love upon my heart and mind that I couldn't help but love him with new abandon and am compelled to tell of it.

The Long Answer

January 2007

I WAS DIAGNOSED WITH MS in mid-June 2006. The results from a spinal tap I had in January 2006 provided the missing piece of the 'puzzle' that my neurologist needed to finally feel confident in making a diagnosis of MS. I haven't looked like a 'classic' MS case right from the beginning, which is why I had to undergo an unorthodox brain biopsy three years ago following inconclusive CT scans and MRI.

In the middle of July, I began taking a medication called Betaseron—an interferon drug I inject every other day. During the first few months, the side effects (mainly flu-like symptoms) were manageable with Tylenol or Ibuprofen and thankfully haven't been a huge issue for me. However, Betaseron hasn't shown any benefits either, and a scheduled MRI later in January will show what course the disease has taken since my last MRI a year ago.

Regardless of what the MRI reveals, my symptoms have become worse since starting on the Betaseron, and disease progression has been insidious these last three years. The rate of decline varies slightly, but the deterioration has been very apparent to me—at times from month to month, sometimes from week to week—and seems to have accelerated since starting the Betaseron six months ago.

To try and tell you what 'feeling worse' means is very difficult. When people kindly ask in passing how I'm doing, I usually give them the 'short answer' and say something like, "Okay" or, "could be worse," or I deflect their question by talking about something our kids or our family has recently done; all in an attempt to dodge the question, which is so difficult to answer. People often tell me that I look good, which is very kind of them, but it's also one of the truly frustrating things about this disease. As of yet, there is no glaring deformity or disability to indicate that anything is significantly 'wrong' with me. But something crucial has been crushed. My symptoms:

- Balance issues; I constantly feel like I'm on a floating dock, and often lean on things for stability.

- My spatial awareness and depth perception are messed up, so I frequently bump into or break things. I often feel crowded and negotiating my way through crowds is a challenge.

- Every step requires thought, and I increasingly avoid crowded places like malls, parties and the church foyer on Sunday.

- Deteriorating eye/hand coordination.

- Numbness and pain in my left hand, arm, shoulder, neck and face— especially in and around my eye.

- Increasing weakness in my left hand, arm and shoulder (My neurologist seemed quite concerned about this.)

- Vision difficulties; it seems like both eyes aren't always focusing on the same thing, like my brain can't decide what to focus on, and my eyes have become photosensitive. Both of these things cause eye pain and headaches.

- Difficulty processing excess sensory stimulation; so again crowds are an issue and Saturdays are sometimes difficult because it can feel overwhelming when all six of us are at home for the whole day.

- Multi-tasking—something I used to be quite good at—is becoming a thing of the past. Frustration sets in if I try to give my attention to more than one thing at a time.

- Headaches; constant sore neck and eyes to varying degrees, most severely in the late afternoon and evening. I've been unable to equalize the pressure in my ears for almost a year now and have constant pain in my temples, cheekbones, and ears.

- Tightness in my throat muscles for three or four months now; this may or may not be related to MS. My sleep is disturbed; usually not too badly at the start of the night, but I wake most mornings around four or five.

- I sense challenges in some of my cognitive functions like concentration and memory, but nothing too serious yet.

Just about all of these symptoms have been with me to some degree since the middle of November 2004; gradually escalating in intensity since then with no sign at all of a remission. I distinctly remember the day, shortly after my return from my brother's wedding in the Cayman Islands, when I felt some tingling in the little finger of my left hand. Within days, the imbalance began and since then every day has been the same or worse in terms of how I feel the disease. It has become second nature to me, and I really don't remember how I felt before all of this.

There are two kinds of MS: relapsing/remitting MS (RRMS), and progressive MS. (PMS). RRMS afflicts almost ninety percent of people with MS, and someone who has it told me that it's the kind you would want to have, if you had to have MS. In June, I was tentatively diagnosed with RRMS in order to secure EDS (exceptional drug status) so I could start on medication. But as time passes, it appears likely that I have progressive MS, which is more difficult to treat. I'm scheduled for an MRI later in January, and then an appointment in mid-February with an interim neurologist who will treat me until a replacement is found for my current neurologist.

I imagine that in February we'll discuss what my options might be in the event that I'm still not responding favorably to Betaseron. Of course, I continue to hope that remission is just around the corner. If or when it becomes evident that I have progressive MS, I suppose I will want to ask many questions about speed of progression, and what I can expect down the road. But I haven't really wanted to think about that a whole lot, so I haven't.

Life is certainly different now, but life is good, because God is good. The Psalm I'm reading this week is 146, "Praise the LORD! Praise the LORD, O my soul! I will praise the LORD as long as I live; I will sing praises to my God all my life long . . . Happy are those whose help is the God of Jacob, whose hope is in the LORD their God." (Ps 146: 1–2, 5 NRSV)

If I lived a hermit's life in a desert somewhere my health issues might be easier to handle in some ways, but I live in a house with five other people (thank God!) and this disease affects us all. God is graciously helping us all to make adjustments. Living with a chronic illness wears me down and renders me intolerant to many things. I am often someone I wouldn't want to live with if I had the choice; an impatient, demanding and at times, belligerent person who sometimes feels she deserves a break because she has a personal challenge to live with. I don't like this person and would like things to be different, but this is where I am—where we are—and truth be told, I don't want to be anywhere else. God is faithful, even though I am not. His promises are sure, so I do not despair. "Whom have I in heaven but you? And there is nothing on earth that I desire other than you. My flesh and my heart may fail, but God is the strength of my heart and my portion for ever." (Ps 73:25–26)

So there you have it; although the result is somewhat vague, this is my attempt to answer the question, "So Colleen, how are you doing?"—a question asked by kind, compassionate people with whom God has graced my life. It is a difficult question for me because there are so many facets to the answer. I realized recently that I have not been communicating very well about how I'm doing, mostly because I don't want to complain (except to my husband, Len—what would I do without him?)

I suppose another reason I've not been communicating well about how I'm doing is because I want to be normal, so I do my best to look and act normal. That being said however, I also don't want to give the impression—at least not to everybody— that everything is just fine. I sense that I need some people to know, as much as is possible, what life is like for me and Len and the kids, to know, if possible, what it's like to be in my skin. That's why I'm writing this missive, to give to people who ask me how things are going, people to whom I don't want to give a simple 'short answer'.

I have often turned for perspective to John Piper's book, *The Misery of Job and the Mercy of God*. In the preface Piper writes:

> It is a great sadness when sufferers seek relief by sparing God his sovereignty over pain. The sadness is that this undercuts the very hope it aims to create . . . ..whatever satan's liberty in unleashing calamity upon us, God never drops the leash that binds his neck . . . pain and loss are bitter providences. Who has lived long in this world of woe without weeping, sometimes until the head throbs and there are no more tears . . . ..but o, the folly of trying to lighten the ship of suffering by throwing God's governance overboard. The very thing the tilting ship needs in the storm is the ballast of God's good sovereignty, not the unburdening of deep and precious truth. What makes the crush of calamity sufferable is not that God shares our shock, but that his bitter providences are laden with the bounty of love.[1]

Some things that I am grateful for:

- The countless prayers said for me, by people I know and by people I don't know.

- The MS did not manifest itself clinically until fairly late in my life. I think of how much more difficult this path would have been ten years ago, when our children would have been that much younger and more physically dependant on us.

- Because substitute teaching has not been feasible for me this year, I have been at home most of the time—something I very much enjoy.

- I am still running, three or four times a week; same route, same pace. I'm stuck in a rut, but it's a lovely loop and I run

1. Piper, *The Misery of Job and the Mercy of God*, 8–9.

it in all seasons. I run solo and there's lots of "elbow space" along the way so bumping into things isn't really an issue when I'm running. I bumped into a parked car once, but it hasn't happened twice! I wear sunglasses and often run with one or both eyes partially closed. I'm usually running mid-morning, when traffic is low. I'm so grateful for my aerobic capacity and the ability to run outside. It's an important 'release' for me, and a wonderful way to think and pray.

- Being at home gives me opportunity to read. I read for short periods of time and during spring and summer I thoroughly enjoyed *The No. 1 Ladies' Detective Agency* series by Alexander McCall-Smith, and more recently *Kite Runner*. Another book I had the time to read slowly and enjoy was *The Pleasures of God* by John Piper, reminding me again of the supremacy of God in all things, and the delight that I am to him. I am currently reading Richard Foster's book on prayer, *Finding the Heart's True Home* and Sigurd Olson's *The Lonely Land*, a true tale of white-water adventure by canoe down the Churchill River.

- I also get to spend much time at home in solitude and silence, a topic that came up frequently in November during a sermon series on 'Sabbath rest.' I enjoyed reading Henri Nouwen's book, *The Way of the Heart,* perhaps because I felt it 'validated' my new 'monastic' lifestyle: "Intuitively, we know that it is important to spend time in Solitude. We even start looking forward to this strange period of uselessness."[2]

Before I sign off, some thoughts I pondered during Advent; John says something that touches us deeply at the distance of the centuries. In unparalleled words he writes with rousing witness, "We declare to you what was from the beginning, what we have heard, what we have seen with our eyes, what we have looked at and touched with our hands, concerning the word of life." (1 John 1:1) How existential is this beautiful phrase of John's, " . . . what we have looked at and touched with our hands . . ." Yes, Jesus, God on earth,

2. Foster and Smith, *Devotional Classics,* 96.

was touched by human beings, handled, gazed on. God is made human in Christ. "God makes himself present to us with such a special presence, such an obvious presence, as to overthrow all the complicated calculations made about him in the past. If Jesus is truly God, everything is clear; if I cannot believe this, everything darkens again."[3]

"Let us therefore approach the throne of grace with boldness, so that we may receive mercy and find grace to help in time of need." (Heb 4:16)

Thank-you for every prayer said boldly on my behalf; each one is important, and cherished.

Love,
Colleen

---

3. Job and Shawchuck, *A Guide to Prayer for All Who Seek God,* 28.

Neurologists

March 2007

I HAVE SEEN TWO neurologists in the last three weeks. My first appointment was with my interim neurologist at the MS Clinic. This visit was a downer for me. I guess my expectations had been too high. The doctor was obviously expecting a quick, straightforward follow-up appointment, not a woman with all sorts of questions about her diagnosis and the efficacy of her medication. I was hoping for some advice, counsel, even an opinion. Instead, he seemed hesitant to give comment about anything. He briefly went over the results from the MRI I had at the end of January, but couldn't tell me anything except that the MRI doesn't indicate whether the Betaseron has slowed the course of disease at all. I left feeling completely inadequate and unprepared to make a reasonable decision about drug options. I went home tired and deflated, and wanted to throw in the towel and not do another blessed thing toward trying to feel better.

A week later, I saw another neurologist and left the office with a weight lifted off my shoulders. He took the time I needed and gave me a much clearer picture of meds than I've had up until now; what they can and cannot accomplish. He doesn't see any viable options to Betaseron right now, which of course is not what I'd like to hear. But, at least he took me through some of his thought processes about my diagnosis, asked me some questions and talked about why it seems we're out of options for now. All this to say that

I felt free to make the decision to quit meds, at least for a time, and walked away with peace of mind. Thank you Jesus, Prince of Peace.

Love,
Colleen

Another Long Answer

August 2007

IN HER ESSAY, 'ON Being Ill', Virginia Woolf wrote:

> English, which can express the thoughts of Hamlet and
> the tragedy of Lear, has no words for the shiver and the
> headache. The merest schoolgirl, when she falls in love,
> has Shakespeare and Keats to speak for her; but let a suf-
> ferer try to describe a pain in his head to a doctor and
> language at once runs dry . . . Pain, in its fracturing of
> an individual self—that is, of relationships between the
> self's different aspects—also fractures that person's re-
> lationships to others just as the impossibility of clearly
> communicating the experience creates a gulf between
> the sufferer and others . . . difficulty describing pain adds
> insult to the injury, yet it seems unavoidable . . . pain's
> resistance to language is not simply one of its incidental
> or accidental attributes, but is essential to what it is.[1]

Lately I've been reading beneficial materials about suffering and
living with chronic illness written by authors who view pain as a
whole-person event, with physical, emotional, psychological, and
spiritual dimensions. The words above are from Kristen Swenson's
book *Living Through Pain: Psalms and the Search for Wholeness*,
and brought me much relief. I have long been frustrated with
my inability to communicate—even to those closest to me—the

1. Swenson, *Living Through Pain*, 40.

nature and extent of my illness; the physical symptoms of my disease as well as psychological, emotional, and spiritual aspects of my illness. So I was glad to read that pain is inherently resistant to language, and that there exists for sufferers an inherent sense of isolation.

The loneliness and isolation that I feel are not crushing, but they are constant. I became aware of feeling isolated and alone shortly after my neurological symptoms appeared. I remember reading at the time, Donald Miller's *Searching for God Knows What*; a book that gave me just what I needed—a picture of heaven to die for. It was one of the things God used to fight the fear that festered in my heart during that Advent season. Miller's book also showed me Jesus in a fresh light, and the realization grew that as much as I love Len, and can't imagine what I would do without him, when it boils right down to it, it's just me and Jesus.

In the darkest hours Len will not be my comfort. Though he will want to be, and would sacrifice much for me, he quite simply will be unable to because he is not Jesus, and only Jesus will do. It's quite a simple thing really, and yet the deeper it seeps into my soul the more staggering it becomes—Jesus and me. It frees me to face aloneness without fear; to face uncertainty without fear, and sometimes even to face fear without fear. It isn't that I am never afraid. At times I am overwhelmed by it. But it doesn't defeat me. A permeating peace keeps the fear in check. God is my defender, "though we stumble, we shall not fall headlong, for the LORD holds us by the hand." (Ps 37:24)

> People around you have no experience that allows them to understand what it means to remain sickly with an invisible disability year in and year out. Invisible disabilities are worse than visible ones. The suffering is masked by a healthy appearance. They are not in wheelchairs and do not use canes. Yet their pain and debility is real and chronic. They have 'invisible disabilities'. It may be the soul-sapping fatigue, environmental sensitivity, and chronic pain of fibromyalgia, or lupus, or lyme disease, or multiple sclerosis. These souls suffer not only from their diseases, but often from the uninformed reactions

of others . . . People with invisible disabilities suffer twice.[2]

Again, I was relieved to read words that echoed another important part of my illness; I appear to be well when I feel like hell. The title of Boyd's book caught my attention, as I had written those words almost verbatim in a May journal entry: "I am afraid. I don't know if I can do this. I don't think I can do this for a very long time, be sick and live well. It seems I'm not as scared to die these days as I am to live, 'dying by inches.' How many inches in a mile? And what if there are still many miles to go? I don't know that I can do it, don't know that I want to do it. Don't know that I can do it well. Christ help me, I am afraid."

At the end of April, I enjoyed a book called *Sacred Rhythms* by Christine Sine. She mentioned a friend of hers who was 'dying by inches' of MS. This didn't sit well with me and for a time I suffered what I'll call a low-grade infection of fear, which was compounded by a return of the general malaise that has been my fleeting companion on and off for about four years now; a sort of restlessness punctuated by sharp uncertainties about the fabric of my faith, a nebulous tension that has found sporadic resolution through different channels of grace.

Within a week of reading the words in Sine's book, I was rescued from an escalating fear by St. Paul's words in 2 Cor 4:16–18:

> So we do not lose heart. Even though our outer nature is wasting away, our inner nature is being renewed day by day. For this slight momentary affliction is preparing us for an eternal weight of glory beyond all measure, because we look not at what can be seen but at what cannot be seen; for what can be seen is temporary, but what cannot be seen is eternal.

These long familiar words of Paul's became vitally fresh for me in May and were the ideal backdrop for Dallas Willard's insights in The Divine Conspiracy, about God's kingdom among us.

---

2. Boyd, *Being Sick Well*, 210, 13.

At times, it seems my illness is sharpening my longing and honing my sensitivity to better see and hear the kingdom among us. My inner self is being 'renewed' and I am experiencing healing. When people ask how I'm doing I'm quick to say that though God is not healing me physically (at least not that I can see) he is healing me in other more significant dimensions. I found these thoughts echoed in Swenson's book. In writing about the nature of pain Swenson looks to the psalms as a model for a holistic suffering, "I distinguish between curing and healing. . . . To be cured, then, is in a sense to return to a former state of being. Healing, on the other hand, happens in any and all acts of making whole. Healing involves the integration of all aspects of a person - physical, psychological, spiritual, and social within that person's present context."[3]

> I have experienced God's healing touch since becoming ill, and isn't that just like him? The low are lifted, the poor are rich, the foolish are wise—be ill to get well. Scriptural juxtapositions that become a voice, a word to reveal Truth in its entirety. Since Advent 2004 the Lord has been good to show me what a mysterious thing suffering is in his hands. There are people who pray for me daily. They pray for physical healing, among other things, and it seems the 'other things' are what God is tending to. I can honestly say that most days I'm good with that, and if I could turn the clock back and have my physical health restored to what it was in November 2004, I wouldn't do it if it meant 'returning' what I have 'gained' since then. There is a dimension now to my life that wasn't there before— or more likely I have simply become aware of something that has been there all along.

My sensitivity to the pain of others is heightened, and my understanding—head and heart—of God's absolute sovereignty has deepened, despite my questions about the authenticity of my faith . . . actually because of the questing.

I am learning a new appreciation for each moment, and how to be present to the present. I have grown accustomed to the gift

3. Swenson, 12–13.

of silence and solitude that my illness affords me. It allows me the space and time to assuage the restlessness and angst I alluded to earlier. In addressing the hermeneutics of pain, Swenson touches on some things that may reflect something of my malaise:

> Perhaps no other human experience so presses us for explanation, so throws us back on metaphysical questions of meaning and purpose as does pain. Furthermore, pain's disruptive nature and the difficulties defining and communicating it call into question one's understanding of one's very self. Pain challenges, chastises, and changes a person . . . Pain calls into question earlier ideas about meaning and demands their reassessment.[4]

I'm so grateful that I've had someone to turn to as I've wrestled with my 'dis-ease'. "LORD to whom can we go? You have the words of eternal life." (John 6:68) And God comes to my rescue as often as need be, tenderly transforming these times of questing into gracious agents of healing. At the end of April, I emailed a friend who wanted to know what my joys and frustrations have been. Many things, I told him, bring me happiness. Joy I shall reserve to mean that moment; scarce and sweet and always a surprise, an enormous bliss, when heaven touches earth right where I am, and I know "All shall be well, and all shall be well, and all manner of things shall be well."[5] (Julian of Norwich) Most days are rich with happiness. There are days, or parts of days, when happiness seems far away, but there is a constant and pervasive peace that remains even when the happiness leaves. "Whom have I in heaven but you? And there is nothing on earth that I desire other than you." (Ps 73:25) Some of my 'happinesses' are:

- My husband, my children, conversations with friends both old and new.

- Time to pray in more reflective, contemplative ways that are new to me.

4. Ibid., 47.
5. Foster and Smith, *Devotional Classics,* 68.

- Books. Although I can't read for long periods of time, I read for short periods and have time to reflect.

- Running. I run three times a week, same route, same pace, and my route allows for lots of space, which I need.

- A recent camping trip to Rushing River with old friends, and the anticipation of our time there again next summer.

All of these things bring me huge collective happiness. I want to embrace, not simply endure, whatever suffering there is along the path I am on, and most days I am able to do that. Having said that, I must also tell you that there are days when I want to scream Frodo's words from The Lord of the Rings, "I wish the ring had never come to me. I wish none of this had happened." [6] And sometimes I do scream them, and God hears me and knows what I can bear and in his mercy, allows no more. I see much wisdom in Gandalf's reply to Frodo, "So do all who live to see such times. But that is not for them to decide. All you have to decide is what to do with the time that is given to you." [7]

I'll spend just a few words on the physical aspect of my health. I have been off of the Betaseron injections for six months now with no positive effect. The progression of disease as I perceive it continues as it did during the seven months I was on the meds, as it did during the 20 months prior to starting the meds. My neurologist at the MS Clinic recently conceded that I do in fact have progressive MS, as opposed to relapsing-remitting MS. All this to say that the arsenal of pharmaceuticals used to treat progressive MS has been exhausted. Betaseron was it. I plan to start taking some glyco-nutrients I've heard good reports about. In the meantime, we continue to adjust to increasing limitations on my physical abilities.

We are in the process of moving. We bought a home in Riverview in June and sold our house last week. The kids have been fabulous in helping Len carry boxes and furniture to the van the last few nights. My vestibular challenges don't allow me to do that

6. Jackson, "The Fellowship of the Ring," DVD.
7. Tolkien, The Fellowship of the Ring, 50.

sort of thing very well anymore. I cut and burn myself, especially my left hand and arm, more frequently as the numbness there deepens. Weakness has also become an issue on my left side and so I rarely use my left hand. I frequently experience stiffness and cramping in my left arm and hand. Tingling and numbness are now constant in my feet and lower legs and, to a lesser degree, in my right hand and arm as well.

The majority of my face is now numb to varying degrees, so if I have food on my face, please tell me! Headaches/neck aches are almost daily, and include eye pain, pressure pain in my ears and temporo-mandibular joints, constricted throat muscles and difficulty swallowing. Vision problems exacerbate my diminished spatial awareness, depth perception, and speed and time–lapse perception. I think what I have the most difficulty with is my increasing inability to concentrate and focus—my 'addled' brain. Deductive reasoning happens at a much slower rate than it used to (no wisecracks here please!) Let's just say that my inherent 'keen sense of the obvious' isn't so keen any more! I find this cognitive vulnerability much more difficult to accept than any of the physical challenges I face.

I began this letter with some thoughts about pain's resistance to language, and find myself back on that topic as I near the end. In Swenson's words, "It is imperative then not only that the person in pain attempt to communicate her experience, but also that others work to understand it. . . . and such witness does not depend on perfectly comprehending the full nature of another's pain."[8]

And so I say thank you, to each one of you who reads this. Your willingness to ask how I'm doing and to hear my answers; the shorter ones I give when we speak, and the longer more exhaustive written ones such as this, means more than you know and play a crucial part in my healing process.

I was recently reminded of how an oyster reacts to a painful grain of sand that gets inside its shell. It responds by wrapping translucent layers around the grain of sand until something of great value is formed. I think an analogy of sorts can be made to

8. Swenson, 42–43.

the pain in peoples' lives. Suffering is indeed a mysterious thing in the hands of God, and the results of suffering can be something of great value. I believe this is not only a possibility in God's kingdom among us, but a definitive dimension of it. I have confidence in a benevolent God, whose love for me knows no bounds and who will continue to allow the transforming effect of chronic illness to draw me closer to him and to produce something of great value. Keeping my eyes on 'what is not seen' allows me to say, "It is well with my soul."

I'll leave you with some words from Psalm 18 that have been a solace for me this week:

> The LORD is my rock, my fortress, and my deliverer, my God, my rock in whom I take refuge, my shield, and the horn of my salvation, my stronghold . . . He brought me out into a broad place; he delivered me, because he delighted in me . . . For who is God except the LORD?" (Ps 18:2, 19, 31a)

Love,
Colleen

What Makes Life Splendid

April 2008

"Children are grateful when Santa Claus puts in their stockings gifts of toys or sweets. Could I not be grateful to Santa Claus when he put in my stockings the gift of two miraculous legs?"[1]

It's April 7, and I have just returned from a breathtaking and life-giving run. Yes, I am still running, and so very happy to be able to do so. Running outdoors in all seasons is one thing that has not changed while so many other things have. The last ten months have been full and fast, owing largely to the buying and selling of houses, followed by moving, renovations and quasi-unpacking. We started looking at houses over a year ago and took possession of our new house at the end of August. I've been in no rush to unpack and there remains much to do before we are settled in, including more renovations this spring and summer.

Having said that, I must also tell you how very content I am here, and grateful for God's permanence in the transience of life. The idiosyncratic nature of time loomed large in my experience this past year—one day a blur and the next a slow trickle of events. We're simply not wired for time are we? Having so much time on my hands, I find myself thinking about it often, and the longer I

1. Chesterton, *Orthodoxy*, 50.

'swim', the stronger my sense that time is less of a river and more of an ocean, and that how I choose to live and attend to each moment is a weighty decision.

"Be attentive to time . . . nothing is more precious. This is evident when you recall that in one tiny moment heaven may be gained or lost. God, the master of time, never gives the future. He gives only the present, moment by moment, for this is the law of created order, and God will not contradict himself in his creation."[2]

I have experienced much happiness since moving to Riverview. I've felt drawn to pay attention to birds, and clouds and skies, to faces, to the heavens and their lights both great and small, and to silhouettes. These are some of the seemingly random things I've felt compelled to notice since the fall, and in doing so I've stumbled happily upon God's coming in arresting ways and in unexpected places.

I recently discovered that for quite some time now I've been living with the false assumption that most of my acquaintances know that I'm not teaching anymore. I was granted disability last May when it became evident that teaching was no longer feasible for me. So rather than teaching this year, I donned a chauffeur's cap in September to take the children to school and back each day. The boys and I dropped the girls off at 8:15am (Victoria's in grade 12, Renee in grade 10) and then Jackson, Nicholas and I had 45 minutes before the bell rang at Laura Secord School, where they're finishing grade six this year. The boys and I spent that half hour before school at Omand's Creek park in our old neighborhood.

On cloudless days during the winter months (and we had many!), our goal was to reach the top of 'Hobbit Hill' before the first rays of sun did. The view across the river buoyed our spirits long into the day, even on the coldest days during Advent.

> *Winter promise hanging in the air over silent river.*
> *Behind stark branches deep in sleep, You speak this Season's hope.*
> *Word of promise spoken from eternity, there's life in death.*
> *For One has come, and comes anew each day,*

2. Johnston, *A Guide to Prayer for Ministers*, 288.

brings life and light to things dead and cold.

Shortly after the first snow fell, Nicholas found a large flattened appliance box on the hill (i.e. refrigerator carton) and five days a week that box careened down 'Hobbit Hill' and 'Penguin Chute' at break-neck speeds, with the boys and I hanging on for some screaming good rides. We incurred only minor injuries and sore stomachs from laughing so hard.

I also joined the boys for lunch every day up until the Christmas holidays. We'd have a picnic in Aubrey Park, and only had to eat in the van two or three times when our fingers were too cold to hold the sandwiches. My boys liked to guess which day I might arrive with a thermos of warm soup. After eating, we'd swing and swing to our hearts' content under a careless blue bowl pouring sun down on us. These lunch hours with my boys brought me huge delight, and even though it's been good all around to have them eating lunch with friends since January, I must say that I do miss those noon hours. Three weeks ago, we bid a fond farewell to our makeshift sled, burying it under the footbridge, and resumed our morning tree climbing and bird watching. We are happy to see the Canadian geese returning, and to hear our own joie de vivre echoed in the vibrant spring chorus at Omand's Creek.

"At present we are on the outside of the world, the wrong side of the door. We discern the freshness and the purity of morning, but they do not make us fresh and pure. We cannot mingle with the splendours we see. But all the leaves of the New Testament are rustling with the rumour that it will not always be so. Some day, God willing, we shall get in."[3]

The last year also brought the deaths of friends and family, both expected and unexpected. These farewells were naturally surrounded by immense sadness, and yet also revealed the rich aspects of Christian community that illness, tragedy and death can conjure. A distant cousin, who travelled to Winnipeg for a funeral, alluded to this richness by suggesting that while many things separate us,

3. Lewis, *The Weight of Glory*, 43.

we all have a strong sense of our Home. And for me, with that strong sense of Home, comes an ever-present Homesickness.

The three family funerals I attended this past year reaffirmed for me that I have an amazing family—"The boundary lines have fallen to me in pleasant places; I have a goodly heritage." (Ps 16:6)—that my 'homesickness' is not unique to me and is, as Lewis puts it, "the secret signature of each soul, the incommunicable and unappeasable want, the thing we desired before we met our wives or made our friends or chose our work, and which we shall still desire on our deathbeds, when the mind no longer knows wife or friend or work. While we are, this is. If we lose this, we lose all."[4]

I was deeply affected by the time I was able to spend with relatives who were anticipating death and grief, as they so beautifully reflected the words of St. Paul in 2 Cor 5: For instance, we know that when these bodies of ours are taken down like tents and folded away, they will be replaced by resurrection bodies in heaven—God-made, not handmade—and we'll never have to relocate our "tents" again. Sometimes we can hardly wait to move— and so we cry out in frustration. Compared to what's coming, living conditions around here seem like a stop-over in an unfurnished shack, and we're tired of it! We've been given a glimpse of the real thing, our true home, our resurrection bodies! The Spirit of God whets our appetite by giving us a taste of what's ahead. He puts a little of heaven in our hearts so that we'll never settle for less.

That's why we live with such good cheer. You won't see us drooping our heads or dragging our feet! Cramped conditions here don't get us down. They only remind us of the spacious living conditions ahead. It's what we trust in but don't yet see that keeps us going. Do you suppose a few ruts in the road or rocks in the path are going to stop us? When the time comes, we'll be plenty ready to exchange exile for homecoming.

---

4. Lewis, *The Problem of Pain*, 151.

But neither exile nor homecoming is the main
thing. Cheerfully pleasing God is the main thing, and
that's what we aim to do, regardless of our conditions.[5]

I stopped taking Betaseron injections over a year ago and the disease has continued its relentless progression. In February, I attended four MS society-sponsored seminars on Primary Progressive Multiple Sclerosis (PPMS). Although some of the sessions were quite rudimentary, it was a good opportunity to be with others (there were eight of us in the seminars) who share some of the challenges I face, but who also deal with other obstacles far more gruelling than my own. At the end of the four two-hour sessions, it had evolved into somewhat of a support group. Of great benefit was a document given to us about PPMS, from the National Hospital for Neurology and Neurosurgery. There is virtually no information to be had about PPMS and it was validating to read about, and not just experience, the unique and unusual nature of PPMS.

I'm learning to partner with my pain and have discovered that one really does adjust to perpetual pain. It has simply become a part of daily life that I've grown accustomed to. Last year, I was cautioned against taking analgesics regularly. So I rarely take analgesics for my headaches anymore nor for the 'aches in my head', pain and pressure in and around my eyes, ears, throat and neck— basically the same kind of pain as I described in August, but more intense.

The cognitive dysfunction continues to progress as well, and particularly bothersome is the visuo-spatial aspect of deterioration. This affects my balance, coordination, and spatial awareness. Caution is always necessary near stairs, heights, or any other situation where my stability is compromised in the least—Talk about being 'on edge'! It also means I'm a poor judge of where I am in relation to people and things around me. Ensuing collisions haven't been serious, though my kids are learning to make a wide berth around me. I frequently collide with inanimate objects that aren't as forgiving as my kids, but so far resulting injuries have been

5. Peterson, *The Message*, 374–75.

relatively minor; bruises, fingers and toes stuck in doors, an oft-bumped head, frequently poked eyes, and some cuts and burns.

> As annoying and painful as these incidents can be, they often generate a reaction of laughter among us, and you can never have too much laughter. I love to laugh, and in fact, come from a long line of laughers. So I was enthralled to read Dallas Willard's insights on the subject: The human condition is one of labour, glory, dust and death. It is one of constant incongruity between human dreams and dignity, on the one hand, and human realities on the other. We are incarnate and finite beings, trailing clouds of overaspiration and ragged incompleteness . . . Laughter is the automatic human response to incongruity, and incongruity is never lacking on the human scene . . . Genuine shared laughter is one of the surest ways for human beings to come together and break the stalemates of life. It is essential to genuine community. No wonder, then, that laughter is so good for our health. It is even a symbol of redemption, for there is no greater incongruity in all creation than redemption . . . Abraham fell on the ground laughing when told by God that he, a one-hundred-year-old man, would have a child by ninety-year-old Sarah. Later Sarah herself laughed at the same 'joke'. God specified to Abraham that the child of promise would be named Laughter. Isaac means 'Laughter.' 'Your wife shall bear you a son, and you shall call his name Laughter, and I will establish my covenant with him' (Gen 17:19). Was this a penalty imposed upon them because they laughed? Hardly. Rather it was a perpetual reminder that God breaks through.[6]

And this is what I find to be true daily; God breaks through the incongruity between my dreams and my reality, between my hopes and my incompleteness. Yes, I do live with the draining reality of this illness and yet I live too, in a kingdom reality that renews me. And God provides much laughter to remind me of the grace in it all.

Numbness is present to some degree throughout my body, and is accompanied by pervasive pain and weakness on my upper

---

6. Willard, *The Divine Conspiracy*, 239.

left side. Though both legs are constantly 'tingling', it hasn't affected my running, other than to alter the sensation of impact on the asphalt and gravel. I sense an encroaching weakness and lack of coordination in my legs from time to time, just a hint of what may lie ahead, and in no way debilitating at this point. The growing numbness in my face worries me somewhat because I feel my ability to smile being affected. I hope that the progress continues in the slow fashion that it has so far, but I do find myself occasionally forecasting a droopy-faced, inexpressive 'me' years down the road, and to be honest, it scares me. Even having to close my eyes occasionally while in conversation is frustrating for me. Our faces are crucial to who we are in relation to others. How can I truly engage in conversation with my eyes closed? But my worries are sporadic and short-lived, because I know that even if I do lose control of bodily movements and functions any loss comes with a choice. "Every time there are losses there are choices to be made. You choose to live your losses as passages to anger, blame, hatred, depression and resentment, or you choose to let these losses be passages to something new, something wider, and deeper." My benevolent Father sustains me with hope that empowers me to make such choices.

My heart went out to Jackie, a woman at the PPMS seminars who choked back tears to speak the words, "My future is hopeless." From time to time when I think of Jackie, I marvel at the hope God sustains me with. This hope gives me a fresh view of his grace, replaces fear with anticipation, and allows me to trust in his sweet sovereignty. Of course the anticipation wavers and there are days when I wonder. I wonder what it might be like to depend on others for transportation. I wonder what it might be like to depend on a feeding tube. I wonder what challenges the pernicious progress of my disease will impose on Len and the children. Some days I wonder if I'll make it to age 60.

But my Rescuer doesn't leave me to dwell on it. "The LORD waits to be gracious" to me (Isaiah 30:18). He comes when I need him most, sometimes in response to the prayers of my friends and family. He comes in creative and sometimes perplexing ways, to make me aware of him. Then I wonder about a myriad of mysteries, and all is well.

As my awareness of God widens, my concept of his sovereignty broadens as well. A few months ago, I settled on the following absorbing words as a framework for my musings about God's will and my will and how the two might meet:

> As I see it, in other words, God acts in history and in your and my brief histories not as the puppeteer who sets the scene and works the strings but rather as the great director who no matter what role fate casts us in conveys to us somehow from the wings, if we have our eyes, ears, hearts open and sometimes even if we don't, how we can play those roles in a way to enrich and ennoble and hallow the whole vast drama of things including our own small but crucial parts in it . . .[7]

Thanks be to God that even when I lose sight of him, he never loses sight of me, and never fails to satisfy, "I am the LORD your God, who brought you up out of the land of Egypt. Open your mouth wide and I will fill it." (Ps 81:10) My prayer is that I will play my small but crucial part well.

Love,
Colleen

---

7 Connor, *Listening to Your Life,* 323.

An Advent Missive

December 2008

IT'S BEEN MANY MONTHS since I last wrote an update. This is mainly because in some ways there is little to bring you up to date on. My health continues in much the same way; a slow relentless deterioration. If I had to limit myself to one sentence, my words to describe it would be, "I am ill, and God is good and loves me exceedingly." Of course, by now you know I will use more words.

We are surrounded by Advent—a time that invokes memories for me of a pivotal Advent season four years ago when I faced great fear and found Jesus waiting to walk through it with me. In late November 2004, my initial MS symptoms appeared, and just days before Christmas I had brain surgery in an attempt to deal with a 'foreign body' that wasn't supposed to be there. I feared it would be my last Christmas with my family, and at times the fear was suffocating, as the days of waiting for biopsy results became many long weeks of the dreaded unknown.

I recall someone telling me they were sorry that such a difficult thing had happened to me, especially at Christmas. My heart's response was to say that there really couldn't have been a better time. The truth of the incarnation shed a remarkable light in my heart that year, and I knew I didn't have to let my fear have the last word because "the Word became flesh and lived among us . . ." (John 1:14). This knowledge kept the blow from crushing me.

Advent is a reminder for me to be glad that Jesus came to earth so that his life could be in me; that God loves me and is in the business of 'repairing' me all the time, and in all the best ways possible. "Your natural life is derived from your parents . . . As long as the natural life is in your body, it will do a lot towards repairing that body . . . A live body is not one that never gets hurt, but one that can to some extent repair itself. In the same way a Christian is not a man who never goes wrong, but a man who is enabled to repent and pick himself up and begin over again after each stumble—because the Christ-life is inside him, repairing him all the time . . ."[1]

Through that December, January, February, and in the ensuing months and years, Christ has come to me time and again, in ways that assure me of the safety in loving God; "to take not a single step without him, and to follow with a brave heart wherever he leads."[2]

Though the progression of disease continues in my body, God keeps pace and fortifies my soul in creative and generous ways. God gives me eyes to see the wonder of life every day. This is a sure deliverance from despair and a natural conduit to gratitude—the best tonic for any ailment. I've been reading Philip Yancey and Paul W. Brand's book, *The Gift of Pain: Why We Hurt and What We Can Do About It* which tells the story of Dr. Paul W. Brand, a surgeon, scholar, investigator and philosopher who spent most of his life among those afflicted with leprosy; a disease that destroys the ability to sense pain. Each page holds relevant material that enlightens and encourages me. In the forward, C. Everett Koop says of Dr. Brand . . . "He opens the window onto new ways of looking at pain . . . to look at pain not as your enemy but as your friend."[3]

I'm beginning to lose my sensitivity to pain, and at times and to degrees, my sensitivity to many tactile sensations. I had an unsettling experience in the late spring when I slammed my thumb in the car door and noticed it only when I tried to walk away and found it was tethered. There was a fair amount of trauma and

---

1. Lewis, *The Beloved Works of C.S. Lewis*, 467–8.

2. Fénelon, *Devotional Classics*, 49.

3. Yancey and Brand, *The Gift of Pain*, x.

throbbing pain took hold later in the day. This happens with less severe accidents as well. Initially they go virtually unnoticed—the pain sensation delayed until later and sometimes not registering at all. Of course, this is not a good thing, and to some degree I understand Dr. Brand's words, "Pain truly is the gift nobody wants."[4] While some parts of my body are becoming less sensitive to pain and various other tactile stimuli, my arms and legs are succumbing to escalating numbness, pain, spasticity and weakness. The most debilitating pain I feel is above my shoulders, daily aches and pressures in my neck, eyes, ears, throat, temples and facial bones. This compendium of pain usually intensifies as the day progresses and fatigue sets in. People and noise often exacerbate the pain and discomfort. This is cause for one of the most difficult adjustments I've had to make. Large group gatherings that used to energize me now drain me, and I find myself hesitating and often avoiding going places and doing things that I once enjoyed. I miss my old self.

I think the human body becomes accustomed to many things given enough time. After a while, one who lives next to the train tracks no longer hears the trains that thunder past. I begin to suspect the same is true with low-grade chronic pain. You begin to not notice it anymore. The plumb line changes and pain simply becomes the perpetual status quo—a mostly unacknowledged part of life. And isn't this wonderful. I think it's a remarkable coping mechanism that God has wired into my body, and I plan to take full advantage of it as long as I am able. I really don't remember what I felt like four years ago, but I know there are parts of many days now when I don't feel 'sick' and I think of myself as a healthy person—albeit with limitations and challenges.

One of the most aggravating things about this disease is that it defies description. "Pain has no 'outside' existence. Two people can look at the same tree; no one has ever shared a stomachache. This is what makes the treatment of pain so difficult. None of us, doctor, parent, or friend, can truly enter into another person's pain. It is the loneliest, most private sensation."[5] Not only is it difficult to

4. Yancey, *When We Hurt*, 20.
5. Yancey, *When We Hurt*, 35.

gauge and verbalize the pain I feel, but perhaps even more difficult to communicate is the effect my illness has on my proprioception; the sense of the relative position of neighboring parts of the body. In a nutshell, it's all out of whack, like having crossed wires. At this point my 'crossed wires' can cause some bizarre and unique sensations. I find I can quite literally follow Christ's command, ". . . do not let your left hand know what your right hand is doing." (Matt. 6:3) At times, my right hand doesn't even know what it's doing. This can bring a strangeness to many activities.

Nonsense
I saw it here but felt it there,
it gave me quite a scare.
I see it there but feel it here,
is this a thing to fear?
Some things are supposed to hurt a lot
And yet I feel them not.
The things they say I ought to feel,
Are these what make up 'Real'?
My hazy questions cast a pall,
the nonsense of it all.
Some day I will be holy whole,
in body and in soul.
I know I'm made for more than this,
I'll feel His healing kiss.

Many people ask if I'm still active, and the answer is yes. I am still running, and was glad to unofficially run the half-marathon in June at the same pace I did seven years ago. There is deterioration in my strength and coordination, so although I hope to run outdoors throughout the winter, I don't want to presume too much.

The cognitive challenges I've mentioned before continue to escalate. Slowed information processing prevents me from responding quickly when a lot of information is presented, and time-sensitive tasks are more challenging; Len and I recently played a scrabble game that took three days.

Screening out distractions such as noise, thoughts and competing activities is a stressful and ongoing challenge for me to deal with. Multi-tasking, or even shifting back and forth between tasks, has become very difficult for me. Coping with unexpected events that require a quick but time-limited response is problematic as well. Visual/spatial functions continue to deteriorate as the disease progresses.

I feel 'lost' in crowds and have difficulty recognizing faces. I judge poorly the distance between objects or people and struggle with imbalance and instability, frequently colliding with things and people. Parking the car is very difficult, and increasingly I'm using handicap spaces to alleviate the stress of trying to park successfully in a regular spot. It's not a physical problem of being unable to walk across the parking lot that prompted me to secure a parking permit, but rather that I experience cognitive problems such as my visual perception and constructional abilities being compromised.

There is a trip to the Mayo Clinic on the horizon. My parents wanted to send me to the Mayo when my health issues first surfaced almost four years ago, and the diagnosis was so ambiguous and long in coming. I put them off repeatedly, thinking resources here in Winnipeg were sufficient, but a few months ago I finally agreed to go.

Arrangements have been made, and I have an appointment at the clinic in Rochester, Minnesota in January of this year. I suppose my parents feel they want to leave no stone unturned in helping me, and I imagine I would share that sentiment if one of my own children were ill. Thank you Mom and Dad for your love. I'm sure the Mayo experience will be fascinating and profitable, and now that things have been arranged, I'm eager to go, though I must admit, somewhat anxious as well. I've grown accustomed to living with a 'mysterious' illness with so many inherent unknowns. What if the 'experts' at the Mayo shed some unfavorable light on some of the mystery?

"We cannot live well without pain, but how do we best live with it?"[6] Dr. Paul Brand asks this important question in the book

6. Yancey and Brand, *When We Hurt,* 26.

by Philip Yancey, *When We Hurt: Prayer, Preparation, and Hope for Life's Pain.* I think the answer to Dr. Brand's question lies in Philip Yancey's words:

> God took on the soft tissue of flesh along with its pain cells just as accurate and subject to abuse as ours . . . By sending the Son to earth, God learned to feel pain in the same way we feel pain. Our prayer and cries of suffering take on greater meaning because we now know them to be understood by God. Instinctively, we want a God who not only knows about pain, but shares in it and is affected by our own. By looking at Jesus, we realize we have such a God. He took on the limitation of time and space and family and pain and sorrow.[7]

Pain comes in all shapes, sizes and colors, and no one is immune to it. When I recall how God has come again and again to rescue me from the penetrating and paralyzing pain called fear, I know that the only way to live well with pain is to look to Jesus. I often read and pray this hymn by Elisabeth Burrowes:

> Thou art the thought beyond all thought, the gift beyond our utmost power; no furthest reach where thou art not, no height but we may find Thee there. Forgive our wavering trust in Thee, our wild alarms, our trembling fears; in Thy strong hand eternally rests the unfolding of the years. Though there be dark, uncharted space, with worlds on worlds beyond our sight, still may we trust thy love and grace, and wait thy word, let there be light.[8]

Advent is a time when God's love and faithfulness are brought into sharp focus for me. Because Christ came my greatest fears are stilled and pain can somehow be infused with purpose.

Love,
Colleen

---

7. Ibid, 119.
8. Job and Sawchuk, *A Guide to Prayer for All Who Seek God,* 297.

Morning Has Broken

March 2009

"True contentment is a real, even an active virtue—not only affirmative but creative. It is the power of getting out of any situation all there is in it."[1]

—G.K. CHESTERTON

IN DECEMBER, I WROTE these words in my Advent missive, "Although I hope to run outdoors throughout the winter, I don't want to presume too much." Well, spring days of increasing warmth and daylight are officially here, and I'm still running outdoors. What an intoxicating season spring is, each day giddy with anticipation of the next. It's muddy and it's full of gravel to be sure, but there is grass under the ice and snow. A spring day breeds joy and contentment like nothing else can.

> In a real sense, an illness is an event with a voice. It is a teacher.
> Seeking healing and recovery is normal and very important.
> Seeking wisdom is even better.[2]

---

1. Chesterton, *A Miscellany of Men*, *http://www.gutenberg.org/files/2015/2015-h/2015-h.htm#link2H_4_0037.*
2. Sine, *Sacred Rhythms*, 185.

These words of Christine Sine's spoke deeply to me a few years ago, and I've recently put them up in a prominent place as a reminder. Thanks to my parents' generosity, I've been able to seek the healing that medicine can offer me. In the middle of January, Len and I made the scheduled trip to the Mayo Clinic in Rochester, Minnesota. My mom stayed at our place for the five days we were gone, and the time away without the children would have been gift enough. We have wonderful children, but I treasured the time alone with Len.

The Mayo Clinic is a sick person's Shangri-La of sorts—a health haven where everything, from every angle, is focused on comfort and recovery. It was a privilege to be there, and a profitable trip all told. I had an MRI that revealed an on-going inflammatory component to my disease and it was strongly suggested that I resume the disease-modifying therapy I stopped two years ago. The MRI also indicated several 'black-holes' (lesions likely indicative of underlying axonal damage) that could explain my lack of improvement these past four years. I was told that this most irregular form of MS is occasionally labelled progressive-relapsing MS, and treatment with interferons would be favored in my case.

For quite some time after our return from Minnesota, I was more confused about my diagnosis and treatment options than before we went. One night was particularly dark, but my Rescuer, answered my prayers and mercifully put my fears to rest.

> "When we are the ones with empty hands, troubled hearts, and confused minds, it is hard to think of new beginnings . . . clinging to hope and light can be nearly impossible. And yet if our feeble faith can reach out to the living God . . . perhaps this is the time when, with anxious hearts and empty hands, we are ready to receive the presence and the power of the One who raised Jesus from the dead. The One who had earlier inspired Mary to say, 'Here am I, the servant of the LORD; let it be with me according to your word.'—Luke 1:38"[3]

3. Job and Sawchuk, *A Guide to Prayer for All Who Seek God*, 101.

Since speaking with my neurologist shortly after we returned, I've come to understand that I would be foolish not to resume therapy as recommended. Though it seems clear that my MS is of a progressive nature, the sub-types within that category are even more difficult to diagnose. As helpful and necessary as labels are, they have their limitations and I mustn't allow the lack of a clearly definitive label prevent me from following the recommendations given by the well-qualified doctors who are caring for me.

So, in early April I will resume Betaseron injections, and as side effects were minimal when I was previously on this drug I am expecting a smooth re-entry. This time around, I won't quit the therapy even though I may not feel any better while taking Betaseron, and even if I continue to feel progressively worse. The medication may in fact be effective, regardless of how I feel. The bottom line is that resuming Betaseron can't hurt me, and it may help me. The hope is that interferon therapy will slow the progression of disease. Although my doctors and I can't know for certain whether or not the therapy is effective, God will know. And this is enough.

> Morning has broken like the first morning
> Blackbird has spoken like the first bird
> Praise for the singing, praise for the morning
> Praise for the springing fresh from the word[4]

Love,
Colleen

4. Farjeon, "Morning Has Broken" in *A Guide to Prayer for Ministers and Other Servants*, 295.

Enter Einstein

September 2009

"Everything that can be counted does not necessarily count; everything that counts cannot necessarily be counted."[1]

SEVERAL MONTHS AGO, I put these words (incorrectly) attributed
to Albert Einstein on our bathroom wall where a captive audience
was sure to read them throughout the day. The sentiment speaks
to something of the fibre of faith—the stuff that gives life depth—
things are so often not what they seem. I can imagine Jesus, with
a twinkle in his eye, saying something along the same lines to his
disciples.

In his 2009 *Christianity Today* article, "Three Gifts for Hard
Times: What I've learned as life has taken a turn for what most
people think is the worst," William J. Stuntz aptly writes about
the pattern of paradox in God's kingdom—a pattern I've become
aware of in recent years:

> That is our God's trademark. Down to go up, life from
> death, and beauty from ugliness: the pattern is every-
> where. That familiar pattern is also a great gift to those
> who suffer disease and loss—the loss may remain, but
> good will come from it, and the good will be larger than

---

1. Cameron, *Informal Sociology*, 13.

the suffering it redeems. Our pain is not empty; we do not suffer in vain. When life strikes hard blows, what we do has value. Our God sees it . . . Jesus' life and death also change the character of suffering, give it dignity and weight and even, sometimes, a measure of beauty. Cancer and chronic pain remain ugly things, but the enterprise of living with them is *not* an ugly thing. God's Son so decreed it when he gave himself up to torture and death. . . . He did not render pain itself beautiful. But his suffering made the enterprise of living with pain and illness larger and better than it had been before. He elevates all he touches. Just as his years of carpentry in Joseph's shop lend dignity and value to all honest work, so too the pain he bore lends dignity and value to every pain-filled day human beings live.[2]

It is correct to say that being numerable carries no intrinsic value. But lately there has been a 'count' that's been important in terms of my health, and that's my white blood cell count (WBCC). I resumed immunomodulatory therapy in April—a course of action recommended by doctors at the Mayo Clinic. Unfortunately my liver hasn't been tolerating the medication well. I've been taking an interferon drug called Betaseron, (the same medication I was injecting three years ago), and my WBCC has been erratic for several months now. Last week it was so low that my neurologist strongly considered having me try a different interferon drug.

I'm slated for an MRI in February and for the time being my blood work is being closely monitored. If my WBCC becomes consistently low my neurologist will prescribe an alternate interferon before the MRI in February. Neither Rebif nor Betaseron are indicated for progressive MS, but as the specific type of MS that I have remains somewhat obscure, the doctors feel some sort of therapy should be employed to try and slow the progression of disease. As my neurologist said, "We're running out of options."

Doctors at the Mayo discussed the unhoped-for eventuality of me not doing well on interferons, or of an MRI a year hence revealing on-going inflammation. This would warrant consideration

2. Stuntz, *Christianity Today*, August 2009, 44.

of escalating to second-line agents that carry low but meaningful risk of serious complications.

There is much about my illness that's uncharted and I'm learning to rest in unknowing. Of course, God is not daunted by my dwindling therapy options and he loves and cares for me regardless of whether plans and choices are stymied or successful.

There's no doubt that I feel progressively worse from day to day. But perhaps I'd be feeling even worse than I do, if I'd not been injecting Betaseron these last six months. Who's to say? When I was on Betaseron three years ago for a time, there was no indication of any positive effects. Then, as now, my condition worsened relentlessly. The progression of disease is inexorable, and at times I imagine myself as an invalid. These projections are clearly futile and I try not to dwell on them. My deterioration is elusive, but I'll try to articulate it as best I can.

There is an encroaching burning and tearing sensation in my limbs and other parts of my body. I liken it to the 'snake bites' we gave each other when we were kids. My friends and I played a sort of reciprocal pain and pleasure game. We were willing to 'take' a snake bite if we could 'give' one. We'd grip the other's forearm in our fists and then twist our hands in opposite directions to effect a painful 'snake bite' in their arm. Something akin to this childhood 'snake bite' sensation is constant in some parts of my body, and makes a sound sleep increasingly rare. It escalates to deeper pain in some areas, and interferes with some daily chores and functions as well.

Coordination in my limbs is diminished, while weakness in my arms and hands escalates. I'm increasingly unstable standing or walking, preferring support, however slight. Sometimes this means holding on to Len or the children when walking beside them, or touching walls if no one's with me. In fact, running is easier than walking because the momentum helps to keep me on course. Persistent muscle cramping in my hands makes writing and other fine-motor skills difficult; and releasing something that I'm holding usually requires deliberate concentration.

My ability to process information continues to deteriorate, and is greatly impeded in large-group settings, so I've become very selective in how much time I spend outside our home. As I've said before, this is the effect of my illness I resent the most. The ear pressure pain and related headaches I've been plagued with for four years now are apparently not MS related, but due to a Eustachian tube dysfunction (ETD) that surfaced shortly after my initial MS symptoms. The specialist I saw last week told me there is no treatment for ETD, and I'll simply continue to use analgesics as required. I've read that Eustachian tube function changes with age, and some disorders may derive from this. I celebrated my fiftieth birthday in July, so I'll just add ETD to my 'things to blame on age' list. On that note, I've found a motto for my next fifty years, "When I was young, I admired clever people. Now that I am old, I admire kind people."[3] (Abraham Joshua Heschel)

I continue to face mounting fatigue each day and am so thankful that disability allows me the time I need to care for Len and the kids. Many housekeeping duties simply take me a lot longer than they used to, and entail potential hazards I must take into account. But truth be told, slowing down has its perks, and I have so much to be grateful for. God's mercies are new each and every morning.

The air is crisp and cool these autumn mornings—perfect for running along a river trail. Only recently have I sensed some wobble and weakness in my legs. Time will tell if and when I must compensate for this. My disease has many inherent unknowns and I'm learning to rest in unknowing. The Lord has shown me time and again that he is sufficient for any fears I might have in the face of uncertainty, dashed hopes, or botched plans. Because God knows all, and is never undone, I am safe. Hamlet says it well, "Our indiscretion sometimes serves us well, when our deep plots

3. Heschel, unkown source, quoted in "Now that I am Old I Admire Kind People. Rabbi Abraham Joshua Heschel." http://www.jewishjournal.com/rabbijohnrosovesblog/item/now_that_i_am_old_i_admire_kind_people._rabbi_abraham_joshua_heschel, line 13.

do pall, and that should teach us there's a divinity that shapes our ends, rough-hew them how we will."[4]

God is. He loves me, ever and always. It is enough.

Love,
Colleen

4. Shakespeare, *Twelfth Night. Hamlet.* 300.

Smooth Seas

October 2009

"Smooth seas do not make skillful sailors."

—AFRICAN PROVERB

I GOT WORD TODAY that my WBCC is at 2.5 again. For those who aren't familiar with blood count figures this is low. This means I will stop injecting Betaseron as of today, and begin the alternate interferon, Rebif as soon as possible.

Five days ago we booked flights to Cayman for January, to visit and dive with my brother Brian and his wife Rocio. I'm asking the Lord for a smooth transition to the new medication over the next three months, so we can make the trip without concerns about my health or meds.

I want to be a skillful sailor, but would love a reprieve from 'rough seas' until we're back from the Caribbean.

Christ have mercy.

Love,
Colleen

The King of the Clouds
March 2010

SINCE I LAST WROTE in September, and just a few weeks prior to our trip to Cayman, I stopped taking Betaseron because my WBCC remained low, and since January I've been injecting Rebif. There were only minor initial side effects when I switched meds, but as with the Betaseron, there has been no clinical improvement in my condition, and instead continued deterioration. But my WBCC seems to be tolerating this medication better, and for this I'm grateful. An MRI in February indicated at least one new lesion in my brain, but since I haven't been taking interferons for some time, it's impossible to say whether the meds are having a positive effect. I will continue using Rebif with careful blood monitoring.

While our time in Cayman was a lovely get away it seems to have coincided with my slope of deterioration becoming more slippery. I really don't think our trip was in any way a contributing factor, but is rather a point of reference as I think about the progress of disease. It felt like all my symptoms—motor, sensory and cognitive, began to progress more rapidly while we were there, but maybe getting away from the daily grind of life simply provided the necessary environment for more astute self-evaluation.

Be that as it may, I confess there are days when I'm unnerved by what seems to be a perpetually steepening slope of progression. I call these 'fade-away days'; days when I feel like I'm sort of 'fading away'. When I do, I sometimes think of Richard Foster's mother

Marie Temperance Foster. Several years ago I read Foster's book, *Prayer: Finding the Heart's True Home*, and very late one night I read the chapter about the 'sanctity of the ordinary'. Foster opens the chapter with a quote by Teilhard de Chardin, "Do not forget that the value and interest in life is not so much to do conspicuous things as to do ordinary things with the perception of their enormous value."[1]

Two pages later, I felt like I'd just read my own obituary, as Foster relates his mother's ambiguous diagnosis of MS and describes in detail her increasing dependence on family members and her gradual physical decline to death. 'Fade-away' days don't come often, but when they do I remember Foster's mother and find consolation in his tender telling of how she honored 'the sanctity of the ordinary' by living an uneventful and ordinary life well, and dying a quiet and ordinary death well. "She loved my father well, and she loved us kids well. She lived through the drab terrain of the ordinary with grace and gentleness. She accepted her slowly deteriorating condition with a noble faith. She received death as she had life and disability: with patience and courage. My mother understood the sanctity of the ordinary."[2]

And so on days when I'm feeling alarmed by what seems to be an increasingly rapid rate of decline, and increasing dependence on Len and the kids, the Lord brings Marie Temperance Foster to mind and I am encouraged to keep plodding along a path of long obedience in the same direction. And although the path is often uneventful and increasingly painful, it's not barren and without happiness. "Pain hurts. That is what the word means. I am only trying to show that the old Christian doctrine of being made perfect through suffering is not incredible. To prove it palatable is beyond my design."[3] (C.S. Lewis) Along the way Christ brings me joy in countless and often unexpected ways. I've found rewarding times of revisiting cherished and often long-forgotten pockets of

---

1. Foster, *Prayer,* 169.

2. Ibid., 170.

3. Lewis, *The Problem of Pain,* 105.

my past; at times by choice, and at other times I'm suddenly and happily there, an appointment by grace.

> *The places we know so well*
> *The places we know so well, where we linger and long to be whole.*
> *A park with some swings where I feel I've grown wings and a peace comes to settle my soul.*
> *Spaces that show us our hearts and draw us closer to home.*
> *Through our stops and our starts, healing our hearts,*
> *there's a Grace that allows us to roam.*
> *Faces speak into our lives of the One in whose image they're made.*
> *And we're desperate to hear so we dare to draw near,*
> *are caught up in the holy parade.*

The path I'm on is certainly not palatable for me, nor for the people who live with me. Everything I've complained of before has intensified. The sensation of burning pins and needles is relentless, affecting much of my body, most recently my eyelids. I am still running although not without misgivings about falling again. My legs have become uncharacteristically sore when I'm standing or walking, and my poor balance exacerbates this. Lack of depth perception and spatial awareness continues to escalate and this, combined with weakness and almost no feeling at all in my left arm, hand and shoulder makes me clumsy and slow. Cognitive challenges continue, most noticeably in my inability to process information well. Lately I've had difficulty planning driving routes. Though the destination is well known to me, I just can't figure out the shortest route to get there. I've driven more miles recently than I've needed to, and have called Len a few times for help. Routine has become increasingly important for me.

I sometimes get the impression that people think sanctification is inherent to living with a chronic debilitating disease; that I am somehow a better person because I'm saddled with this illness. I'm not. William Stuntz, a man in the grip of overwhelming physical and emotional pain and suffering speaks to this misconception, ". . . illness does not beget virtue. Cancer and chronic pain make me sick; they don't make me good. I am who I was, only more diseased."[4] Stuntz goes on to say that rather than removing life's curses, God redeems them.

Though I first read these words by Philip Yancey long ago, I've been mulling them over during Lent as they so poignantly speak essential Easter truth, "He (Jesus) took on the limitation of time and space and family and pain and sorrow . . . In the resurrection that followed his death on the cross, he transformed the nature of pain. He overthrew the powers of this world by first allowing sin to do its worst, then transmuting that act into his best . . . God takes the Great Pain of the Son's death and uses it to blot up into himself all the minor pains of our own confinement on earth . . . The pain of humanity has become the pain of God."[5]

"'Christ's luck to you, sweetheart!' Colman cries. 'Happy be she that wings where the wind wills knowing it blows fresh from the mouth of the King of the Clouds! Happy be she that leaves it to God where her feathers fly her!'"[6] "There is only one way to love God: to take not a single step without him, and to follow with a brave heart wherever he leads."[7] Whether it's spoken in Brendan's Gaelic tongue, or Fénelon's French, the truth is that what's essential for a long obedience in the same direction is to follow Jesus Christ, and it is God who makes me brave to do so. Left to myself I cower, but when I trust the King of the Clouds then I am strong, surrounded by God who loves me, who goes with me.

So despite the 'fade-away' days and increasing disability, there is joy along the way. There is God-given depth to every day. As Buechner says, "Faith is a way of looking at what there is to be seen in the world and in ourselves and hoping, trusting, believing against all evidence to the contrary that beneath the surface we see there is vastly more that we cannot see."[8] God's love knows no limit.

---

4. Stuntz, "Three Gifts for Hard Times," 44.

5. Yancey, *When We Hurt*, 119–21.

6. Buechner, *Brendan*, 105.

7. Foster and James, *Devotional Classics*, 49.

8. Buechner, *Secrets in the Dark*, 70.

In the Abbreviated Psalter of the Venerable Bede, Psalm 15 reads, "Guard me, God, for I have trusted in you, saying to God: You are my LORD; it is not well with me without you."[9]

May it be well with you.

Love,
Colleen

9. Brown, *The Abbreviated Psalter of the Venerable Bede*, 25.

The King of Love

October 2010

THANKSGIVING—I THINK THIS IS a good time to write an update as I have much to be grateful for. Although my deterioration continues without pause, it is progressing slowly, so I'm not driven to desperate measures like some others who have travelled to distant places in search of relief from their MS. Perhaps I too would be heading to Poland, Costa Rica or Mexico if I weren't still able to do many of the things I want to.

Though it's not precipitous, there is a stable daily decline in the cognitive and physical areas that have been affected for the last six years. This dictates increased caution in many areas of my life, and I have become more so in the kitchen recently after burning both arms on separate occasions. Though my legs feel increasingly heavy and simultaneously numb and painful, thankfully the only walking aids I have had to use are the walls, a banister or a friend's helping hand. My waning limb strength and dwindling balance frighten me at times, but I'm very thankful to still be running.

The MS landscape in general has been anything but constant for the past year since Paulo Zamboni went public in November 2009 with his potentially paradigm-shifting theory that CCSVI (chronic cerebrospinal venous insufficiency) could be associated with MS. I want to convey my own personal perspective on the ensuing turmoil caused by Zamboni's hypothesis, and on the intricacies of the controversy surrounding CCSVI. In March I was despondent because I hadn't been accepted to participate in any of clinical trials I'd applied for. By April my initial elation over Zamboni's breakthrough had been replaced by a healthy scepticism. The more I heard and read, the more apparent it became to me that the CCSVI theory was quite speculative in nature. I had nothing but daunting questions and no idea how to proceed or even how to think about it all. But in his usual timely fashion, the Lord brought me consolation through these words that I much needed to read:

> To feel fear is not unusual and sometimes it is a necessary and life-saving experience. Fear alerts us to the dangers that could harm us or even take our lives. However, when fears dictate all our actions, we can become paralyzed and incapable of thinking clearly or living faithfully . . . Ever since Jesus appeared to the disciples, Christians have discovered that there is no need for fear when one is in the presence of God. To walk with God not only rebukes our fears and sends them away but also increases our courage.
>
> To walk with God is to be reassured of direction, guidance, and strength for our daily journey. What do we have to fear when we are in God's presence and care? Nothing at all! This does not mean that we will be spared discouragement, disease, or death itself. It does mean that we will never be alone. It means that we will be given strength to meet the demands of our daily lives. It means that we will receive wisdom to judge wisely and well in the directions we must take. It means that we will know the joy and tranquility of living in the presence of God in every circumstance of life. From fear to courage is the natural journey of all who walk with God.[1]

In spring, I read the journal of Chris Klicka, called *My Power Perfected in Weakness*. Chris died after a fifteen-year battle with progressive declining MS. His book was a tonic—a brilliant reminder that sickness and not even death are the worst that could happen to us.

1. Job and Sawchuk, *A Guide to Prayer for All Who Seek God*, 185.

For a few reasons (one being that sources I trust do not recommend it) I have no thoughts of pursuing CC-SVI testing and treatment. Time will tell, and only the King of love knows the outcome for the 'MS world' and for me. Julian of Norwich said it well with her strong, simple words, "All shall be well, and all shall be well, and all manner of things shall be well."[2]

Once again, thank you for listening.

Love,
Colleen

---

2. Foster and Smith, *Devotional Classics,* 68.

God is Good

December 2010

God is good, all the time God is good.

GOD'S MOST RECENT KINDNESS to me was a phone call I received from the MS clinic yesterday morning telling me that my most recent blood work was aces and that my neurologist is so pleased with it, that I get to keep all of my blood till March! This was welcome news since my WBCC has been erratic since August and I was beginning to fear a recommendation to change to higher risk medications. Once again, the sweet Lord has come in a way and at a time I didn't expect him.

"If we are to experience God, we must be open to God, to the mystical, to the divine, appearing in our lives. And we must have an openness that is free of any preconditions about how that will happen. Looking for God in a godly form is the great historical mistake."[1]

Love,
Colleen

---

1. Hays, *In Pursuit of the Great White Rabbit,* quoted in Job and Shawchuk, *A Guide to Prayer,* 379.

New Year, New Pain, New Prayer

January 2011

WELL WE'VE JUST BEEN given a new year . . . and about three weeks
ago I got notice in the mail that I've also been given a new neurologist. My doctor is leaving to focus on his work elsewhere, and I've
been transferred to a new doctor. I'm to plan for a longer than
usual visit at my initial appointment in May, as he will be review-
ing my MS treatments and history in detail. To a large extent, my
treatment and care are based on the information I give the doctors
about how I'm feeling, so please pray that I'll be able to give a lucid
account in that regard. And on the topic of prayer . . . I've been
mulling over some thoughts during the past few months that I'd
like to run by you. I've called this update "New Year, New Pain,
New Prayer" and I'll use this title as a starting point to try and
elucidate some of the scattered thoughts that have led me to think
about a new approach to prayer with regards to my health.

I have been wondering if prayer is more potent when it's focused
on a smaller more restricted 'target'? In other words, are specific
prayers more potent than vague prayers? Are informed prayers
more effective than general prayers?

When I pray, I think I feel more effective if I'm armed with
some details to pray about. But that being said, there are often times
that I pray without knowing the particulars . . . and certainly times
when my supplications sound more like an SOS distress signal.
More often than not, it is at these times that I carefully consider to

whom I am praying—God Almighty, Maker of heaven and earth. And I am immediately at peace to plead with him in my ignorance. I am convinced that all my prayers, silent or spoken, are entirely the King's initiative, and this conviction brings me huge happiness. C.S. Lewis articulated this mystery well in his words:

> Master, they say that when I seem to be in speech with you, since you make no replies, it's all a dream—one Talker aping two. They are half right, but not as they imagine; rather, I seek in myself the things I meant to say, and lo! the wells are dry. Then, seeing me empty, you forsake the Listener's role, and through my dead lips breathe and into utterance wake the thoughts I never knew. And thus you neither need reply nor can; thus, while we seem two talking, thou art One forever, and I no dreamer, but thy dream.[1]

Surely I can trust God to sort through all my prayers for anything that might be of benefit. I think I may have exuded an inordinate amount of enthusiasm in the short update I sent out a month ago about my 'Aces' blood work, and my doctor's satisfaction with my WBCC. It was good news, but I'm afraid my update may have led you to believe that things have somehow vastly improved for me. It was so nice to have something even remotely positive to report.

The not-so-good news is that nothing has changed in terms of how I feel, which is ever more poorly and my disease continues to progress. The perceived pressure in my ears remains constant, contributing to my escalating head, neck, throat and facial pain. Some days my head feels unbearably 'heavy' and I wonder if this is because of the pain in it or because my neck muscles are weakening. The 'good news' I received simply means I can continue taking the same medication I have been for a year now, and don't have to consider trying a new therapy.

I included New Pain in the title of this update because in the last few weeks I have noticed the presence of a new persistent 'hurt' in the plague of pains. My left shoulder and neck have become relentlessly painful. At times I'm acutely aware of pain on the surface

1. Lewis, *The Wisdom of C.S. Lewis*, 39.

of my skin, while at other times (and sometimes simultaneously) I sense a sharp hot stabbing pain deeper in the muscle bed. The shower spray causes a searing sensation, while certain arm and head movements bring the deeper sharper pain. Either way, the 'new pain', and the inexorable 'old' pains are limiting, and have brought me to greater reliance on family members. I'm thankful to still be driving, but gripping the steering wheel, in fact simply touching/holding anything, causes a similar searing sensation in my hand, arm and shoulder, predominantly on my left side at this stage. I surmise the 'new pain' is simply another step on the path to paralysis.

Shortly after noticing the pain in my neck and shoulder, I started to have thoughts about a new plan, a different approach to praying about my illness. The thought came to me, "Wouldn't it be a treat to have just one pain diminish or disappear? Maybe I should ask those who pray for me to pray for 'less' . . . to ask the King for a 'small' reprieve from just one of the plethora of pains, rather than asking him to remove multiple symptoms." But then I wonder if I am, in some way attempting to manipulate the Almighty by suggesting this new approach to prayer. I spoke this thought to a wise confidant who suggested that I ought to think of it not as manipulation, but rather as an experiment. And what if a reprieve isn't granted?

There are so many questions and ambiguities in this business of prayer and healing aren't there? Frederick Buechner wrestled well with them, and wrote some wise words that have brought me consolation time and again:

> Whatever else it may or may not be, prayer is at least talking to yourself, and that's in itself not always a bad idea. Talk to yourself about your own life, about what you've done and what you've failed to do. And about who you are and who you wish you were and who the people you love are and the people you don't love too. Talk to yourself about what matters most to you, because if you don't, you may forget what matters most to you.
> Even if you don't believe anybody's listening, at least you'll be listening. Believe Somebody is listening. Believe

in miracles. That's what Jesus told the father who asked him to heal his epileptic son. Jesus said, 'All things are possible to him who believes.' And the father spoke for all of us when he answered, 'LORD, I believe; help my unbelief!'(Mark 9:14–29).

What about when the boy is not healed? When, listened to or not listened to, the prayer goes unanswered? Who knows? Just keep praying, Jesus says. Remember the sleepy friend, the crooked judge. Even if the boy dies, keep on battering the path to God's door, because the one thing you can be sure of is that down the path you beat with even your most half-cocked and halting prayer the God you call upon will finally come, and even if he does not bring you the answer you want, he will bring you himself. And maybe at the secret heart of all our prayers that is what we are really praying for.[2]

And so, perhaps we can ask the King to diminish just one aspect of my illness. But which one do I suggest we pray about? Well I'm not exactly sure. If we are, in some sense, collaborating in a 'prayer experiment', it's perhaps best to avoid targeting my cognitive decline, as detection (and description) of any improvement might prove more difficult than improvement in my physical pain or discomfort.

Triaging the pain is not easy. As disturbing and painful as the 'new pain' is, the 'older' escalating pains I've complained about for so long, particularly the ear pressure pain, may in fact take a greater toll. So I'm going to suggest that my head pain (ear pressure and associated neck, throat, head and facial pain) be the focus of our prayers over the next few months. I shall do my best to pay attention well, and to give a candid account of any reprieve I experience. And if no reprieve comes, of this I am certain—the King will help me come to terms with it, and will bring me to wholeness in his perfect timing and faultless fashion.

Even when God intervenes mightily, such as melting a tumour within minutes or pouring miraculous spiritual comfort on breathtaking pain, healing is still a process, one that continues as long as

2. Buechner, *Wishful Thinking*, 86–7.

you are alive to God's presence. You can expect an awareness of God's presence to break into your life many times. God continually invites you to yet another step toward wholeness.[3]

Love,
Colleen

---

3. Job and Shawchuck, *A Guide to Prayer for All Who Seek God,* 223.

Happy Spring

April 2011

THANK YOU FOR YOUR generous responses to the 'ramblings' I sent you in January, and for being receptive to my 'prayer experiment' suggestion. I'm grateful for your charitable words that were such an encouragement to me! But when I read words like "strength of character, faith and long suffering, and heroic approach," I decided I needed to set the record straight. I am no saint, and to be candid, I often do not graciously accept my lot in life. As my disease progresses, I find I am intermittently cross with God, and there are times I'm raging mad at him. A song on Steve Bell's "Devotion" CD spoke volumes to me when I first heard it a couple of years ago. Even the song's simple title, "He Will Know," is a tender tonic. I remember pandering to self-pity not long ago and saying out loud, through tears and clenched teeth, "So you know do you? Yet you do nothing to make life just a bit easier for me in SOME way!" I was upset. And in his mercy God listened to my rant, and then came and restored peace to my angry heart. I recently said to an old high school friend, "My faith is small and my strength precarious . . . but the one I put my faith in, he is a rock. Any vitality or strength you perceive in my life is a grace given me by Jesus Christ."

In her perceptive book, *An Altar in the World*, Barbara Brown Taylor wrote words that I found particularly incisive . . ."Pain is provocative. Pain pushes people to the edge, causing them to ask fundamental questions such as 'Why is this happening?' and 'How can this be fixed?' Pain brings out the best in people along with the worst."[1]

Some of my 'worst' is thinking that because I got 'stuck' with fast-fading health, I should be entitled to a few breaks in some other areas of life. I've become acutely aware of the fact that pain drains, and have frequently entertained thoughts like . . . "God, can't you at least see to it that we don't have any more vehicles breaking down?!" (We've had a run of vehicle problems lately.) I know that this inane line of thought can be detrimental to relationships, and I want no part of it . . . especially when I find myself trying to justify my poor treatment of those I love by thinking, "With all the pain I live with, who could blame me for being short-fused?' Wrong! I know it's wrong, absurd and dangerous, and I would value your prayers in this regard . . . that I won't indulge self-pity. I don't want to become a bitter person. I want to be someone on whom nothing is lost. In light of the fallacious thoughts that subtly penetrate my mind and skew my judgement I need to be mindful of the bounty in my life.

Yes, I was overwhelmed by your kind responses to my last update, but right after sending it I also struggled for a time with regrets for having sent it, because I felt foolish for suggesting that you pray in a certain way for me. At the beginning of my update I said that I believe prayer is God's initiative, and two pages later I suggested you pray in a specific way for me. So I wrestled for a while with this ostensible contradiction. These thoughts combined with some insights I'd read about Job made me fear I'd behaved presumptuously. Did I think I was God, telling you how to pray for me? And for a while, and probably for good purpose, I felt apprehensive about the 'prayer experiment' I'd audaciously suggested, and worried that the whole thing might be offensive to God. I told him so, and in the intervening weeks, he brought me to a peaceful place, nourishing me with fine thoughts about prayer, first and foremost these of Richard Foster:

---

1. Taylor, *An Altar in the World,* 156.

> There is no better way to learn about prayer than by pray-
> ing. . . . It is good to debate the mysteries of prayer, to
> ponder the profundities of prayer, to learn the methods
> of prayer. It is better to pray. Prayer is a little like an auto-
> mobile: you do not have to understand everything about
> its inner workings for it to get you somewhere. I have
> found that if we simply pray—even if we pray in wrong
> ways—God is pleased with our feeble efforts and Jesus
> lovingly guides us into more excellent ways. Also, we can
> be assured that the blessed Holy Spirit will adjust, cor-
> rect, and interpret our prayer before the throne of God.[2]

The Lord was kind to use Foster's insights to remind me that our
smallest efforts at prayer are managed and magnified by the Holy
Spirit and are made fit for the throne room.

In regard to how I've been feeling, I have to tell you that there
have been no improvements. If anything, the progression of disease
has been more insidious than ever in the last couple of months.
Never before have I thought of a wheelchair as an actual possibility, but perpetual pain in my legs and feet at different levels (i.e.
'burning' at the surface level and stiffness and aching at a deeper
muscular level) and decreased ability to walk and run well, have
recently made me consider that the likelihood of needing a walking aid of some sort is very real, and may be more imminent than
I'd ever imagined. The pain in my arms and hands is incessant,
and manual dexterity continues to decrease. More often I need assistance with many menial tasks and this frustrates me to no end.
The 'new pain' in my left shoulder and neck that I mentioned in
January, has joined the ranks of the incessant 'old pains' and made
room for other new pains. And the pain in different parts of my
head (ears, neck, throat, jaws, and face) hasn't waned. So there you
have it . . . another downer update. I wish it could be different, but
for now anyway, it's not.

Since some have asked me recently about CCSVI treatment,
I'll say that I have no inclination to pursue that treatment because
from what I've read, those with RRMS experience more symptom

---

2. Foster and Smith, *Devotional Classics,* 131.

relief after undergoing the experimental procedure than do those with progressive forms of the disease.

In light of having to tell you again, that there's no improvement in my health, I also want to say that though it may appear that God isn't present in the situation, he most certainly is, and it's often been in his apparent absence that I've found him to be most present. I've long loved Frederick Buechner's perspective on Job:

> It is out of the whirlwind that Job first hears God say, "Who is this that darkens counsel by words without knowledge?" (Job 42:3) it is out of the absence of God that God makes himself present, and it is not just the whirlwind that stands for his absence, not just the storm and chaos of the world that knock into a cocked hat all man's attempts to find God in the world, but God is absent also from all Job's words about God, and from the words of his comforters, because they are words without knowledge that obscure the issue of God by trying to define him as present in ways and places where he is not present, to define him as moral order, as the best answer man can give to the problem of his life. God is not an answer man can give, God says. God himself does not give answers. He gives Himself, and into the midst of the whirlwind of his absence gives Himself.[3]

In her book *Chasing Grace*, writer and clinical psychologist Martha Manning writes, "There seem to be two levels of suffering. There's the suffering itself. And then there is the almost universal sense of isolation that comes with the territory of suffering. The sense of being apart in one's pain . . . has to do with the hard but true fact that no one can walk our road for us."[4] But she goes on to say:

> I have also learned that I don't have to go through every type of pain to make me a credible listener. I have no intention of becoming an alcoholic so that I can better understand those members of my family, friends, and patients who struggle with alcoholism. I pray that I am spared from that, and all the other hardships that would

3. Buechner, *Telling the Truth*, 43.
4. Manning, *Chasing Grace*, 97.

make me closer kin to other sufferers. In my own way I have suffered long and hard, and it has taught me that there are also universals of pain that can bridge the gap between my experience (or lack of it) and another person's very different pain . . .

The essence of the singular struggle with suffering is the same. It is the dogfight between spirit and strength on the one side and fear and resignation on the other. We all know the universals of the struggle: it's hard, it's lonely, it's scary, and it takes too damn long."[5]

Manning then relates an old Irish legend that soundly illustrates the premise "that just having a companion on some part of the road can make the long, lonely walk seem shorter, and make the journeys, however difficult, infinitely more bearable."

Thank you for the companionship that this writing and reading of updates creates. It truly does make the walk seem shorter, and the journey more bearable.

Looking forward to Easter and the celebration of all things made new.

With love and gratitude . . .
· Colleen

5. Ibid, 98–9.

My Proverbial Update

September 2011

"He who lives medically lives miserably."

—LATIN PROVERB

·

TRUTH BE TOLD, I was quite miserable immediately after my May appointment with my new neurologist. In response to my last update in April, two friends of mine, a doctor and a nurse, recommended that I either start taking medications for neuropathic pain or talk to my doctor about making adjustments to my medication, if I was already taking something. Peripheral neuropathy causes damage to the peripheral nervous system that causes pain, numbness, tingling and/or muscle weakness in the extremities.

Up until that point, I didn't know that medication specific to neuropathic pain existed, so I was eager to discuss treatment options with my doctor. But when I brought up the topic, he offered no advice or information at all. I was disheartened to say the least. More than once during the appointment, he made reference to how well I was doing, and said that I was expecting too much. The next day, after discussing our impressions of the visit, Len and I agreed that we both heard him say that he doesn't feel I have primary progressive MS because I still walk so well, but neither did we hear him offer an opinion as to what type of MS I do have, other than to say it's highly irregular. My misery was relatively short-lived however, because it compelled me to go back and look at the reports I got from the Mayo Clinic almost two years ago. After re-reading them, it became clear that my new neurologist and the one I saw at the Mayo certainly agree that I don't have PPMS. While it's clear that neither doctor is certain about the type of MS I do have, their uncertainty has reminded me that my Father in heaven knows, and that's far greater consolation than having the correct medical label. Both doctors also seem to agree that the initial onset of my symptoms in November 2004 was representative of an acute attack of demyelination and the underlying axonal damage (nerve cell destruction) that occurred in that attack explains my lack of improvement. Both doctors are also resolved that I continue on Rebif, the interferon medication I inject three times a week.

Two weeks after I saw my neurologist I went to see my general practitioner. That visit proved to be more fruitful and I am currently trying medications that I hope will soon bring some relief from neuropathic pain, in particular from chronic paresthesia (the persistent pressure, prickling and burning sensation that I experience in my feet, legs, hands, arms, face, and other areas of my body). My GP also suggested I drink tonic water, as the quinine it contains may help alleviate the muscle spasms in my legs.

A few months ago I read a book called Timeless Healing, about the integration of body, mind and soul, and often found myself agreeing with Benson's view that our physical well-being is closely linked to many aspects of our beliefs, values, thoughts and feelings. The proverb I started with in this update is from his book, and serves as a reminder to me that there truly are weightier matters in life than my physical health. Although the progression of disease in my body is relentless, I know that things could be much worse than they are. Many of my cognitive and physical abilities are still intact, and for this I'm grateful. I know too, thanks in part to some of the responses to my last update, that what I suffer due to MS pales in comparison to the pain that many others endure. Physical deterioration and pain seems a far lighter load to bear than the heart-wrenching pain of broken relationships that I read about.

I face my days carried by Len's love, the care and support of treasured friends and family, and by the persistent prayers of many people. Time and again, the strength God provides through these relationships bolsters me and prevents self-pity from having the upper hand in my heart. I was reminded of this when I read these words in Benson's book . . . "when you go on with your life, giving your full attention to each person and situation rather than allowing yourself to settle into a quagmire of burdens, your body is motivated to forget illness and pain, . . . and to remember the strength and vitality associated with your full experience of life."[1]

While reading about the pain in others' lives, my own pain is put into proper perspective, and again I realize how rich I am. In his book *Free of Charge*, Miroslav Volf beautifully articulates how I want to live my days:

> "If the presence of the gift-giving Christ makes us rich, rest will replace weariness, and peace will banish unending restlessness. Like the apostle Paul, we will then know the secret of being content whatever the circumstance . . . A rich self has a distinct attitude toward the past, the present, and the future. It surveys the past with gratitude for what it has received, not with annoyance about what it hasn't achieved or about little it has been given. A rich self lives in the present with contentment . . . it is "always having enough of everything" (2 Cor 9:8). It still strives, but it strives out of satisfied fullness, not out of the emptiness of craving. A rich self looks toward the future with trust . . . because it believes God's promise that God will take care of it."[2]

Last week, someone asked me if I've been able to enjoy running in the fabulous weather we've been having, and I was grateful to be able to say, "Yes." I have fallen twice since I last wrote, but I haven't sustained any serious injuries. In my previous update I suggested

1. Benson, *Timeless Healing*, 266.
2. Volf, *Free of Charge*, 109–10.

that I was stumbling more frequently while running, due to my increasing inability to flex my ankles. Now I know that the reason for my stumbling, and for the falls, is that I am simply not lifting my legs high enough. As they become weaker I'm having difficulty lifting them high enough to clear the asphalt every time I bring my foot forward. And when I don't, I take a tumble. But I think abrasions, bruises and sprains are a small price to pay for the physical and mental benefits I derive from running outdoors. Running and walking are both things I need to do with increasing diligence as strength and dexterity dwindle and pain persists. Lately however, I've begun to wonder which I'll lose first, my mobility or my ability to use my hands and arms. How happy I am to have five extra pairs of able and obliging hands close by.

I began with a Latin proverb, and I'll end with a sacred one, "The human spirit will endure sickness; but a broken spirit—who can bear?" (Prov 18:14)

So be it. It is well with my soul.

Love,
Colleen

A Word From the Trenches

December 2011

ALTHOUGH I REALLY DON'T enjoy waiting for many things in life (who does?), the waiting aspect of Advent is something I anticipate each year. Advent waiting doesn't focus alone on Jesus Christ's return at the end of time, but is also a time of waiting and watching for Christ to appear in my own life today. And he does, at times in astonishing ways if I have eyes to see it. Seven years ago during Advent, I began a two-month wait for brain biopsy results, and with each day of waiting the fear grew that I wouldn't live to see another Christmas. They were critical weeks for me, my mortality crashing into my consciousness every day, and many nights.

> *Fear*
> *Wells up from below . . .*
> *Fear of the unknown . . .*
> *Fear of the known.*
> *Gag to quell it.*
> *Gulps of tears to drown the fears.*
> *The key of release from the stifling cage . . . Breathe.*

But through the days of Christmas and through to mid February, a peculiar peace settled in my heart and in our home, and at times the memory of it brings me to tears. Seven years later, the crisis of having to consider tumours and cancer is long past, but the peace has not passed. The peace that carried me through crisis seven years ago has carried me through chronic illness in the ensuing years, offering a kind of 'chronic' wellness . . . a steady presence that permeates all areas of my life, so that my physical decline doesn't define who I am. Christ's presence is powerful and paves my way with a peaceful perspective that colors everything. C.S. Lewis's words in The Weight of Glory ring true for me, "I believe in Christianity as I believe that the sun has risen; not only because I see it, but because by it I see everything else."[1]

When I wrote an update in September, I mentioned that I was trying some medication that I hoped would bring some relief from neuropathic pain. Initially I took a low-dose anti-depressant for several weeks that did nothing for my pain, but did make it very difficult for me to get up in the morning. And for the last several weeks I've been taking an anticonvulsant that is supposedly quite effective in treating neuropathic pain. I've yet to sense any improvement, but will continue on the meds for a few months in the hope that eventually I will. The possible side effects listed for both drugs include some of my existing MS symptoms: drowsiness, dizziness, loss of coordination, tiredness and fatigue. I will need wisdom to weigh the benefits of the meds.

I've recently read The Gift of Pain by Dr. Paul Brand, world renowned hand surgeon and leprosy specialist, which served to counter encroaching self-pity. The book is the fruit of Brand's many years of working with people who suffered from pain and people who suffered from the lack of it. The diverse responses to pain of people from England, America and India informed his thoughts over many years. Though not a pain expert, Dr. Brand's vast experience allows him to write about more than just managing the pain associated with leprosy. The book came out of the conviction that, in his words, "Most of us will one day face severe pain . . . and the attitude we cultivate in advance may well determine how suffering will affect us when it does strike."[2] The book was a tonic for me, and reading it refreshed my perspectives on several fronts, and perhaps most importantly made me grateful that I'm challenged

---

1. Lewis, The Weight of Glory, 140.
2. Yancey and Brand, The Gift of Pain, 12.

by MS rather than by a much harsher neurological disease like lep-rosy. Neuropathic pain comes in an assortment of sizes and colors, and these are some of mine:

- Allodynia is pain, generally on the skin, caused by something that wouldn't normally cause pain. Examples of allodynia are pain caused by mild pressure from clothing, a light touch, gentle massage, or sheets rubbing against the skin.

- Dysaesthesia comes from the Greek word "dys" meaning "not-normal" and "aesthesis" which means "sensation" (ab-normal sensation). It's an unpleasant and often painful sense of touch caused by lesions in the nervous system, peripheral or central, and for me it involves sensations, both evoked and spontaneous, of burning pins and needles, as well as icy coldness.

I experience the pain of Allodynia and Dysaesthesia in my feet, hands, legs, arms, face and eyes and parts of my back. Besides the surface, or skin pain, my neuropathy also manifests itself at a muscular level, causing weakness and cramp-like pain deep in my muscles, mainly my legs and arms. My legs, more so the left, feel like logs and a slight limp at times seems to be how my body is dealing with this. And yet, I'm still running without a limp. I've not fallen recently and for this joy in my life I give God thanks. My chief grievance is the fact that my neuropathic pain is without respite.

C.S. Lewis was no stranger to both physical and emotional pain and I appreciate his perspective from *A Grief Observed*:

> What is grief compared with physical pain? Despite what fools may say the body can suffer twenty times more than the mind. The mind has always some power of evasion. At worst, the unbearable thought only comes back and back, but the physical pain can be absolutely continuous. Grief is like a bomber circling round and dropping its bomb each time the circle brings it overhead; physical pain is like the steady barrage on a trench in World War

One, hours of it with no let-up for a moment. Thought is never static; pain often is.[3]

I thought Lewis's trench analogy characteristically incisive; and true and tender his perspective on God's apparent silence when Lewis questions him about suffering, "When I lay these questions before God I get no answer. But a rather special sort of 'No answer.' It is not the locked door. It is more like a silent certainly not uncompassionate, gaze. As though He shook His head not in refusal but waiving the question. Like, 'Peace child; you don't understand.'"[4]

There certainly are fragile days when God seems silent and dangerously distant from my plight, but the sense of well-being remains even so and I am grateful that his peace keeps pace with the challenge of living with the chronic as it did with the challenge of facing the critical.

Thank you for taking time once again to read. I am grateful for your prayers. I wish for you and yours the peculiar peace of Christ, and much joy in your Advent waiting.

"By the tender mercy of our God, the dawn from on high will break upon us to give light to those who sit in darkness and in the shadow of death, to guide our feet into the way of peace." (Luke 1:78–9)

Love,
Colleen

---

3. Lewis, *A Grief Observed*, 40–41.
4. Ibid., 69.

A Large Reality

March 2012

"We shake with joy, we shake with grief. What a time they have, these two housed as they are in the same body."[1]

WHEN I CAME ACROSS the above words in a poem by Mary Oliver, I was struck that someone had so concisely and creatively captured the tension I live with; a struggle between distress about my illness and joy in any number of things I become aware of when I relax my hold on my rights and open my eyes to my wealth. I think it's a tension common to all, between fighting and accepting what life hands us. The truth is, sometimes I wonder why God doesn't just FIX me. But in the words of Wendell Berry, "Reality is large, and our minds are small."[2] So I choose to live in the large reality of my life.

I find it's so much easier to let Jesus, my wise and faithful companion, sort out all the loose ends I often struggle with. I'm learning that rather than use my small mind to shrink reality in attempts to figure things out, it's much more relaxing, and fun, to let the One who knows the big picture manage things. It's also much more likely that in doing so I will recognize moments of grace,

1. Oliver, *Evidence*, 13.
2. Berry, *The Way of Ignorance*, 132.

and the 'pleasant inns' he provides. To be honest, it's difficult and at times even boring to continually write (as I suspect it is to read) about my declining health and to try and articulate details about my body's deterioration. So I've chosen to use C.S. Lewis's words as a springboard for this springtime—almost Easter update:

> The Christian doctrine of suffering explains, I believe, a very curious fact about the world we live in. The settled happiness and security which we all desire, God with-holds from us by the very nature of the world: but joy, pleasure, and merriment, He has scattered broadcast. We are never safe, but we have plenty of fun, and some ecstasy. It is not hard to see why. The security we crave would teach us to rest our hearts in this world and op-pose an obstacle to our return to God: a few moments of happy love, a landscape, a symphony, a merry meeting with our friends, a bath or a football match, have no such tendency. Our Father refreshes us on the journey with some pleasant inns, but will not encourage us to mistake them for home.[3]

The most recent 'inn' on my journey was a vacation in the Ca-ribbean. You'd think two weeks surrounded by sea, surf and sun would be an obvious 'pleasant inn' and an exceptional time of refreshment. The snorkelling was indeed a delicious distraction from life in Winnipeg, but the fact that I came home less refreshed than I could have led me to a Lenten lesson.

I know that the Caribbean 'inn' would have been all it was meant to be for me if I'd been more deliberate in focusing on the many things I could enjoy rather than brooding about the incon-venience of ongoing renovations where we were staying. But God is gracious, and despite my poor attitude there were many mo-ments of joy because he showed himself to me time and again, in countless and often surprising ways.

As my physical deterioration persists, so does fear of the un-known, and God has graciously given me another 'inn' recently that is providing philosophical refreshment; a book by Samuel

---

3. Lewis, *The Problem of Pain*, 116.

Wells called *Be not Afraid, Facing Fear with Faith*. Early in the book, Wells relates a short anecdote about waiting in a buffet line, noticing the struggles of the young woman in front of him who's just learned that her crutches will be a life-long necessity, and asking her, "How on earth do you manage with the crutches and all the inconvenience?"[4] She answers Wells, "You get used to it. You can get used to almost anything after a while."[5] As my mobility becomes increasingly tenuous, it was heartening to read these words that echoed the thoughts I expressed some three years ago in my update What Makes Life Splendid . . ."I'm learning to partner with my pain and have discovered that one really does 'adjust' to perpetual pain. It has simply become a part of daily life that I've grown accustomed to."

Half a year later, I referred to this adjustment as a coping mechanism that I think God in his mercy has hard-wired into my body. That having been said, I am still hoping that my chronic neuropathic pain, musculoskeletal pain and paraesthesia, will soon respond to the meds I've been taking. I have my annual appointment with my neurologist in May. The MS clinic protocol is to have patients complete a questionnaire at every visit. I detest this questionnaire because most of the questions have little to do with my progressive relapsing condition and the rest of the questions involve grading individually, on a scale of one to ten, my ability to perform any number of daily functions and then grading the pain and difficulty I experience in doing so. It was a relief last year to discover an answer near the end of the questionnaire that encapsulated well the self-diagnostic answer that I will opt for in May, "Everything is now harder to do."

It requires considerable concentration, but I am still able to run. Although it's been several months since I've fallen while running, in Cayman the girls watched as I took an innocuous but embarrassing tumble while standing right next to Len.

In his chapter on healing, Wells presents a lucid explanation connecting healing and salvation, and closes the chapter with these

4. Wells, *Be Not Afraid*, 21.

5. Ibid., 21.

astute words, "So the question, does God heal? can only be asked alongside the question, does God save?" And these are the answers Wells suggests "Does God heal me? Sometimes. Does God save me? Always. Always. Always."[6]

Hallelujah! The blessings of Easter to you!

Love,
Colleen

6. Wells, *Be Not Afraid*, 14.

Playing and Praying

June 2012

I WAS SOMEWHAT TAKEN aback recently when someone asked me what the day-to-day was like for me, and so failed to give a satisfactory answer I'm sure. And if any of you wonder about my daily grind, I don't know that I can tell you anything about it other than what I've long told you, "Even though on the outside it often looks like things are falling apart on us, on the inside, where God is making new life, not a day goes by without his unfolding grace."[1] Of course days going by speak of time, but Frederick Buechner's words remind us that time isn't measured in strictly linear terms. "We tend to think of time as progression, as moment following moment, day following day, in relentless flow, the kind of time a clock or calendar can measure. But we experience time also as depth, as having quality as well as quantity—a good time, a dangerous time, an auspicious time, a time we mark not by its duration but by its content."[2] And what better content for any of our days or hours than the myriad expressions of God's unfolding grace.

A recent unfolding of his grace in my life was the realization that playing and praying are a powerful, and at times inseparable pair. I chose long ago to believe that time spent playing is time well spent, and a most genuine way for me to love God. Kierkegaard

---

1. Peterson, *The Message*, 374.
2. Buechner, *The Faces of Jesus*, 14.

said, "We create ourselves by our choices."[3] And I think there is much truth in this. I have often acted on my belief about play, perhaps at times to a fault. Play often has a serendipitous slant that makes it very much a "living in the present" unfolding of grace, if you know what I mean. To help explain my meaning I will borrow words from CS Lewis, "Never, in peace or war, commit your virtue or your happiness to the future. Happy work is best done by the man who takes his long-term plans somewhat lightly and works from moment to moment 'as unto the Lord.' It is only our daily bread that we are encouraged to ask for. The present is the only time in which any duty can be done or any grace received."[4] How this played out in my life recently was the skydiving that contributed hugely to my overall sense of wellbeing and was oh so much fun, but far too soon over. Prayer came into play here, as many who knew of my plan to jump from a plane didn't share my enthusiasm and felt compelled to pray for me, bless them.

On a more serious note about prayer, I appreciate Henri Nouwen's perspective, "Prayer leads you to see new paths and to hear new melodies in the air. Prayer is the breath of your life that gives you the freedom to go and stay where you wish and to find the many signs that point out the way to a new land. Praying is not simply some necessary compartment in the daily schedule of a Christian or a source of support in time of need, nor is it restricted to Sunday morning or as a frame to surround mealtimes. Praying is living."[5] I think if my living involves much playing, then my playing is, in a sense, praying. Since I started sending out updates about my health more than five years ago, and hearing back from some of you, I've come to understand in new ways the universality of pain, and the possibility of purpose in it.

> *The Prism of Pain*
>
> *A web of pain weaves through our lives to show there's much we share.*

3. Oliver, *Evidence*, 6.

4. Lewis, *The Weight of Glory*, 61.

5. Nouwen, *With Open Hands*, 80.

The anguish of untimely death, too much, too much to bear.

The slow, relentless draining wait for only God knows what.

Deflated hopes held too high drip silence in the night.

Dreaded deep of darkest night, and fear of fiendish fear.

The crush of betrayal, the slap of deceit, unspoken words no one will hear.

We are none of us alone in our pain.

The pain of the past and the pain of now, the pulse of your pain echoed in mine.

Holy hues refracted in the tear-stained faces of the prism of pain.
"Blessed be the God and Father of our Lord Jesus Christ, the Father of mercies and the God of all consolation, who consoles us in all our affliction, so that we may be able to console those who are in any affliction with the consolation with which we ourselves are consoled by God." (2 Cor 1:3–4)

Play and prayer, channels of grace, at times inseparable, and both generous gifts to any day. I hope always to play and pray in earnest.

Love,
Colleen

The Lapse of the Year

October 2012

The Lapse of the Year
Spring am I, too soft of heart Much to speak ere I depart:
Ask the summer-tide to prove
The abundance of my love

Summer looked for long am I
Much shall change or ere I die
Prithee take it not amiss
Though I weary thee with bliss!

Laden Autumn here I stand,
Weak of heart and worn of hand;
Speak the word that sets me free
Nought but rest seems good to me

Ah, shall Winter mend your case?
Set your teeth the wind to face
Beat the snow down, tread the frost,
All is gained when all is lost."
(William Morris)

These words are on a tea towel that I've periodically hung in my kitchen for years, but this fall they've stirred my imagination in a peculiar way. I suspect this is so because I've long felt that Morris's words allegorically reflect the lapse of my life, and this fall I am more than ever feeling weak of heart and worn of hand. Printing and writing demand my careful concentration, and my left hand and arm are virtually useless—weak, numb, and painful while at rest, as well as when I try to use them. For some time now, I've sensed increased 'confusion' in my nervous system, a waning of my ability to sense, interpret and respond to my immediate physical surroundings. I think I became aware of a more rapid progression in my deterioration even before we left for Europe in mid-August, and I fear the slope of my decline may have steepened while we were away. My limp is certainly more pronounced, and pain more profuse.

I enjoyed a gorgeous fall-free autumn run today, much more satisfying than my run three weeks ago that ended with a fall on the asphalt. At times it seems my brain can't differentiate messages sent and messages received, resulting in occasional mishaps. Our month in Europe was brilliant, though I felt dreadful more often than not, and struggled to maintain balance and pace as we walked and climbed the characteristically steep and cobbled roads and sidewalks of Europe. Our days spent in the leather markets of Florence, and Rome's Colosseum and Forum come to mind as being particularly challenging, while at the same time exhilarating! Italy was as captivating as I'd remembered it. I do wonder if my attempts to tackle the European terrain exacerbated my condition, or if I've simply reached a stage of disease I'd be at regardless, and an age I'd be at regardless. I often speculate to what degree the natural aging process is to blame for my pain. Of course I can't know the answers to these questions, but what I do know is that my family's tender attentions to my increased need for help are precious. I don't mean to make light of any loss when I say that over time I've come to believe that if we have eyes to see it, even when good things are lost to us, other good things, at times even better things, sometimes fill the void that is left. Though a harsh winter is imminent, I still maintain my appreciation for the change of seasons in Winnipeg, and whether The Lapse of the Year reflects the passage of twelve months or many years, my tea towel serves to remind me that God's hand is in it all, and his love graces each season with unique and bountiful beauty. For this I am grateful.

A happy autumn and Thanksgiving to you and yours.

Love,
Colleen

Abe and Simon

November 2012

I BELIEVE IT WAS Abraham Lincoln who said, "Most folks are about as happy as they make up their minds to be."[1] Now and then I try to imagine what it would be like to wake up one morning feeling 'normal'. I try to remember what that felt like, and I can't. But believing that it could happen brings me joy, because I also believe that it's not my belief, nor the strength of my belief, that will muster the miracle. My heart often echoes the cry of the boy's father in Mark 9:24, 'I do believe, help my unbelief.' I sense no pressure to believe. I sense simply the privilege of believing, as best I can, that a miracle can happen in my life. "The miracle that breaks the rules reminds us that the rules themselves are miraculous. We need to rediscover and cherish a basic sense of wonder, of surprise, of the precariousness of actuality. In Ecclesiastes, the dismal world-weary preacher of the Old Testament might grumble that, 'there is nothing new under the sun' (Eccl 1:9), but the New Testament answers loudly and excitedly, 'Look! I am making all things new' (Rev 21:5) Of course, we all may sometimes experience Ecclesiastes moods, and if we do, it is comforting to know that they are not outside of God's domain. However, we should not devote our minds and imaginations to prolonging and justifying them. We should aim rather to have minds and imaginations ready to respond joyfully to the truth that in Christ everything is given

1. Source unknown.

back its youth and at least something of the freshness of the very first days of creation."[2]

As Advent approaches I'm reminded of the miracle that happened when God put on flesh in Bethlehem, and Jesus Christ was born. Now, if God could do that he can certainly heal me. Will he? I don't know. I can't say that I believe he will, but I do say that I believe he can. That belief coupled with the knowledge that he knows my name, makes me happy. And my belief in the Bethlehem baby coupled with the knowledge that he loves me is the source of my hope. "Hope makes it possible to look beyond the fulfillment of urgent wishes and pressing desires and offers a vision beyond human suffering . . ."[3] (Henri Nouwen)

Yesterday was a whiner day. I didn't hesitate to complain to Len about all that ailed me. His comment to me was, "It seems to me Col, that some days are better for you than others."

"Better?," I said. "Well in the sense that they're not worse than the day before, yes I suppose they are. Every day is as bad as or worse than the day before. That's what progressive relapsing MS is like." "Well then maybe some days you're able to cope better than others," he suggested. "Yes, I think that's true," I agreed.

I suppose the days when I'm tired of coping, tired of being tired, and tired of taking increased yet ineffective pain medication, are my "whiner" days. And the days when I buck up and cope are my silent "better" days; days when I make up my mind to be happy, carried by the joy that comes from believing that a miracle could happen in my life because I'm known and loved by the Master of miracles—days when hope helps me look beyond the fulfillment of my wishes and desires to see that my life, though marred by illness and selfishness, is indeed marked by miracles, and full of grace and goodness beyond telling.

As Christmas comes close, may you and yours know grace and goodness beyond telling.

Love,
Colleen

2. Job and Shawchuck, *A Guide to Prayer*, 295.
3. Nouwen, *The Wounded Healer*, 76.

Meandering Miracle

March 2013

AFTER I SENT OUT my November update I was compelled to read and re-read my update in hopes of discovering what I'd written to invoke so many generous responses. I say this because I sometimes feel I get the credit that rightly belongs to God and to you good people who collaborate with him through your prayers. I was afraid that I'd inadvertently given the impression that my circumstances are intolerable. My circumstances are not unbearable. I bear them, as could anyone else. God consistently gives me what I need when I need it, a principle I believe to be consistent with God's Kingdom.

What I live with is more sufferable by far than the incomparable pain in many others' lives. Pain is common to all of us but I'll take my pain any day over some other kinds of pain. Inevitably, with each update I've sent out, I've a had responses that speak of others' pain, and this has been a good thing for me. It brings to mind Richard Foster's wisdom about confession, "Confession is a difficult discipline for us because we'll too often view the believing community as a fellowships of saints before we see it as a fellowship of sinners."[1] What is true for sin is also true for pain. If we hear of another's pain it can free us to speak of our own pain. A year ago, in my update entitled "Happy Spring," I made mention of Martha Manning's thoughts about the universal struggle with suffering, "the dogfight between spirit and strength on the one

1. Foster, *Celebration of Discipline*, 145.

side and fear and resignation on the other,"[2] and I'm certain her words ring true for those suffering pain of any sort. The plethora of pain that recently became evident in the lives of people dear to me prompted me to listen to the invaluable perspective of Peter Kreeft on the topic of evil and suffering. When elucidating the philosophical problem of evil, he speaks to the fact that bad things happen not just to bad people but to good people.[3] Kreeft makes some logical suggestions about the benefits of pain, and suggests that people who live almost totally pain-free lives become simple stupid shallow little selfish pigs. Or as Rabbi Abraham Heschel, one of the wisest men of the twentieth century once said, "The man who has not suffered, what can he possibly know, anyway?"[4] Listening to Kreeft helped me come to terms with my suffering and with the suffering of people dear to me.

I made mention in my last update of my belief that God is undoubtedly able to heal me, while also recognizing that he may choose not to. Early in the year, I came across some wonderfully thought-provoking words by Frederick Buechner on the topic of miracles, "A cancer inexplicably cured. A voice in a dream. A statue that weeps. A miracle is an event that strengthens faith. It is possible to look at most miracles and find a rational explanation in terms of natural cause and effect. It is possible to look at Rembrandt's Supper at Emmaus and find a rational explanation in terms of paint and canvas. Faith in God is less apt to proceed from miracles than miracles from faith in God."[5] Though I'm not entirely sure of Buechner's meaning, his words gave me pause to again consider miracles and what they may or may not be. Though I've said it before, I feel I need to say it again; God is in the process of healing me though I can't attest to any improvement in my physical state. For six-and-a-half years my experience has mirrored this textbook description of Progressive Relapsing MS: "PRMS is the

2. Manning, *Chasing Grace,* 99.

3. Kreeft, "The Problem of Good and Evil," *YouTube* video, 15:40. May 27, 2104. https://www.youtube.com/watch?v=W2NmwGG0XPE

4. Ibid., 33:40.

5. Buechner, *Wishful Thinking,* 74.

rarest course of MS, occurring in only about 5% of people diagnosed. People with this form of MS experience steadily worsening
disease from the beginning. They do not experience remissions in
the sense that patients with RRMS do."[6] And so, always reaching
for a wall or banister, especially in crowded areas or when the surface is uneven, I fumble and stumble, and tumble and grumble my
way along as my balance deteriorates and my neuropathy remains
resistant to a variety of ineffective medications. But though I've
experienced no remissions or a cessation in my decline, don't you
think my 'stamina', my ability 'to focus on the good rather than the
bad', 'to hope rather than despair', 'to cope well', 'to remain happy
and hopeful', to be willing to 'keep the faith', and to 'recognize that
God can heal, but may not'; don't you think these things, all said
by friends and family in response to my last update, are indicative
of a grand work God is doing? I'd like to think so, and to think of
them as a meandering miracle . . . where the healing isn't physical,
but is targeting more important matters of the mind and heart that
can only be addressed under the present circumstances of illness.
"Everywhere a greater joy is preceded by a greater suffering."[7] (St.
Augustine) Someone suggested that how I walk the path I'm on is
the result of my deep walk with Jesus. But I know that how I walk
the path I'm on is the result of Jesus' walk with me. From Steve
Bell's song, "Descent" he is, "Weak, to be with [me] when [I] fall
and strong to save." When I face a loss I don't face it alone. Jesus'
strength allows me to be vulnerable as I grieve the losses and suffering that my illness brings. His strong presence lets me patiently
hope that there is wisdom to be gained through losing, and that
there might be purpose in my pain.

6. MS Answers, "What is Progressive MS?", lines 49–53.

7. Augustine, *The Confessions by St Augustine*, book 8, *145*.

Songbirds and Old Sayings

July 2013

I SPOKE WITH MY neurologist in early June and was given his sanction to titrate down the Gabapentin I've been taking for many months. By August I'll be medication-free but for my tri-weekly Rebif injections, a relatively simple facet of my life and much less likely forgotten than taking variable numbers of pills at various times of the day. I've been taking Gabapentin for well over a year, with no reprieve from neuropathic pain.

The pain is part of who I am. The ever-present 'surface level' neuropathic pain is a sensation of hot penetrating pins and needles, and is encroaching upon increasingly more areas of my body. Every walking step I take is akin, I imagine, to walking on hot thumbtacks and when running more intensely so.

My hands, wrists, arms, torso and face are all under the same duress; and always the left side of my body more acutely so than my right. The 'deeper level' pain—the muscular aching—is constant in my legs, arms and hands, and my left hand is particularly prone to assuming a claw-like position.

My neurologist has asked me to consider taking another medication, Cymbalta, with many of the same possible side effects as all of the others I've tried, as well as some other potentially more unpleasant ones. If I decide to try Cymbalta, it will be the fifth medication that I've tried, in hopes of alleviating neuropathic pain.

I'm sick of making decisions, tired of weighing consider-
ations, sick of taking capsules, tired of FORGETTING to take capsules; and many days, just sick and tired of being sick and tired.

I've just returned from a run without spotting any eagles. No
offense to Isaiah, but when I run alongside the riverbank, it's on
the wings of the songbirds that I rise, their chorus a clear credit to
their Creator and a tonic for me. Apparently I limp not only when
I walk, but also when I run, or so I've been told. Yet I've averaged
only one fall a year during the last six years, running regularly
three times a week, outdoors in all seasons. This is a gift I marvel
at, and I deem it worth every bit of pain needed on my part to
have. The privilege of being able to run outdoors year round is
something I don't take for granted.

As my body succumbs to the malevolence of MS, I must make
certain in my mind that if I permit it, my Creator will give purpose
to my pain; and trust that in the picture he sees, my pain is not
in vain. "We are fallen like the trees, our peace broken, and so we
must love where we cannot trust, Trust where we cannot know."[1]

How long will I be able to run, or to walk for that matter? I
don't know the answers to those questions. The fear of not knowing what the future holds for us can be very strong and unless a
way is found to ease it, that fear can overwhelm us.

In the movie *The Best Exotic Marigold Hotel*, the optimistic
Sonny offers comfort to an agitated friend who fears the unknown
future with these words: "There is an old saying that says, 'Everything will be all right in the end', so if it is not all right, it is not yet
the end."[2]

Sonny's 'old saying' made me smile because in it I heard a
Hollywood paraphrase of Julian of Norwich's wisdom that has
bolstered me for many years: "And all shall be well and all shall be
well, and all manner of thing shall be well."[3]

---

1. Berry, *Sabbaths*, 83.

2. Parker, Ol and Deborah Moggach, *The Best Marigold Hotel*, DVD,
23:50.

3. Foster and Smith, *Devotional Classics*, 68.

There are days when I am cantankerous about my pain, think it definitely not all right, and wonder to what point my pain will escalate before it is all right. Then I recall how blessed I am to know that the God who loves me is someone I can trust when not knowing.I found solace recently in these words by Richard Rohr:

> It becomes sacred space, and yet this is the very space we avoid. When we avoid darkness, we avoid tension, spiritual creativity, and finally transformation. We avoid God who works in the darkness—where we are not in control! Maybe that is the secret. . . . the pain . . . is not forever; there is a light and you will see it. This isn't all there is. Trust it. Don't try to rush through it. We can't leap over our grief work. Nor can we skip over our despair work. We Have to feel it. That means that in our life we have some blue days or dark days. Historic cultures saw it as the time of incubation, transformation, and necessary hibernation.[4]

Thinking back and looking ahead as I tend to do these days with my birthday drawing close, I see that for quite some time I have perceived a desire—a need—to pay attention, but to precisely what I'm not certain; other than to perhaps the moment at hand. And I wonder if each new day we wake to doesn't deserve the same fanfare that the turning of our years does. If there is truth in the words of these saints and lovers of God then perhaps it is so. "You will find the living God in the pages of the Bible. You will find him also just exactly where you are . . . He leads through all the events, all the circumstances of your life. Nothing in your life is so insignificant, so small, that God cannot be found at its centre."[5] (Mother Frances Dominica)

Love,
Colleen

4. Job and Shawchuck, *A Guide to Prayer for All Who Seek God*, 102.
5. Job and Shawchuk, *A Guide to Prayer*, 15–16.

A Pilgrim's Progress

October 2013

"God is great, God is good, let us thank him for this food. Amen."
—TYPICAL CHRISTIAN MEALTIME GRACE PRAYER

THROUGHOUT MY CHILDHOOD, THIS was the prayer we said before every meal. As thanksgiving approached this year it frequently came to mind, as well as a renewed conviction of gratitude's galvanic quality, and of the simple truth that if I am to live my life well I will live it gratefully. "Rejoice always, pray without ceasing, give thanks in all circumstances; for this is the will of God in Christ Jesus for you." (1 Thes 5:16–18)

I find the words "in everything give thanks" easier to swallow when I remind myself that 'in' does not mean 'for'. Being thankful for everything is a challenge I've found difficult to meet. But being thankful in everything doesn't seem such a tall order, because the bounty in my life is so big it's not difficult to be thankful even when the bounty is at times overshadowed by lean times; and especially so when all I have to do is look at front page news, or down the street, or across the city, to see that the bounty I've enjoyed all my life is, by and large, non-existent in most peoples' lives.

We find by losing. We hold fast by letting go. We become something new by ceasing to be something old. This seems to be close to the heart of that mystery. I know no more now than I ever did about the far side of death as the last letting-go of all, but I begin to know that I do not need to know and that I do not need to be afraid of not knowing. God knows. That is all that matters."[1]

Buechner's words, especially when read in context of his stimulating essay, "A Room Called Remember," are ripe with philosophical truth about death, but I've put them here simply because for me they also reflect a practical truth that I've come to appreciate in recent weeks. The phrase, "We find by losing," became significant this summer as I slowly weaned myself off the apparently ineffective gabapentin I'd been taking for two years. By the end of July, when I was finally 'clean' of gabapentin, I'd come to realize that although gabapentin had been ineffective in removing my neuropathic pain, it had certainly reduced its intensity. But I'm not sure I would have 'found' that truth had I not first 'lost' all neuropathic pain restraint.

By August, I'd come to the conclusion that I did not want to endure unbridled neuropathic pain if medication was available to at least curb its intensity, so I decided to try cymbalta. When I saw my neurologist three weeks ago it was evident that the upshot of taking cymbalta was only unwelcome side effects, and we simultaneously concurred that a return to gabapentin was my best option. At present, having been on full dose for just three weeks, I've yet to notice any decrease in my neuropathic pain, but I expect that with time I will.

During the last several months the nature of my pain has changed somewhat in that while the neuropathic pain is persistently present 24/7, the musculoskeletal component of my pain has increased, meaning I've become aware of more pain in my muscles and joints than previously. This aspect of MS—spasticity—is both a sustained stiffness as well as random leg spasms at night that feel like a sudden and severely painful tightening of my muscles. Regardless, it is my neuropathic pain that the Gabapentin is meant to alleviate. My neuropathic pain affects the left side of my body to

1. Buechner, *A Room Called Remember*, 189.

a greater degree than my right side, and is something I'm always mindful of except when I'm asleep.

Allodynia is a particularly painful sensation in response to a normally innocuous stimulus such as a light touch, bed sheets or clothes. It is usually short-lived and lasts only as long as the stimulus remains.

Dysesthesias is a burning, aching, itching sensation that has been described as feeling as if there is acid under the skin. I call these sensations 'hot spots', and have felt them with increasing frequency in the last while. It may be triggered by a light touch or by nothing at all. The "pins and needles" sensations often fit into this category.

T Francois Bethoux, MD describes this baffling, complex, often debilitating pain as, "an illusion created by the nervous system . . . The nerves are too active and they send pain signals with no good reason—they're firing a pain message when they shouldn't be."[2] ·

In MS, damage occurs to the myelin sheath; a layer of fatty protein that protects the nerves and aids transmission of messages. Nerve messages can be interrupted or delayed, interfering with the body's normal ability to function. Sometimes the brain interprets these disrupted messages as pain, even though there is no physical cause of pain.

In my case, MRI's indicate several 'black-holes' or lesions, likely indicative of underlying axonal damage and not merely myelin sheath damage. This explains my lack of improvement and insidious decline since 2004, and substantiates my diagnosis of progressive relapsing MS.

My balance continues to deteriorate, as does my ability to navigate while driving or walking.

What I hope to learn from Buechner's words is to be grateful for whatever is on my plate, regardless of my circumstances, so that if it should one day not be there, I won't regret not having valued it. And I have many things to be grateful for. Even under

2. Carcione, "Pain and Multiple Sclerosis," lines 21, 24–5.

the pall of MS, the list is long; close to the top being my sustained ability to run outside.

God is great, God is good. Let us thank him. Amen.

Love,
Colleen

A Party

January 2014

EVEN THOUGH I'VE NEVER made a New Year's resolution, I recently received a bookmark with words on it that reminded me of, and reinforced, my long-held conviction about how best to live my life. The words are Frederick Buechner's: "The grace of God means something like: Here is your life. You might never have been, but you are because the party wouldn't have been complete without you. Here is the world. Beautiful and terrible things will happen. Don't be afraid. I am with you."[1]

I want to remember that the world I live in is the party, and I'm an important guest every day. The party will have an element of unpredictability as all parties do, and although not all that happens at the party may be pleasant, the party promises to be of phenomenal proportions, none of which I need ever fear for the party host is ever near.

Some unpleasantness I've already experienced this year is the escalation of last year's neuropathic pain. I spent much of my last update giving account of that and so will now say only that it hurts, the pain's not killing me, and things could be worse. Not everybody can say that, so I count myself blessed, knowing I have naught to fear and will best rest in that knowledge if I live each part of every day to the fullest, anticipating and appreciating whatever it may hold to bring me closer to the heart and purposes of God.

1. Buechner, *Wishful Thinking*, 39.

How do I do this I ask myself? But for the grace of God I don't know. But I think speaking it helps bring it to pass.

I'm off to the hospital shortly for an MRI. I don't expect it, but should anything noteworthy show up you'll hear from me after my follow-up appointment with my neurologist.

Love,
Colleen

High Midsummer Pomps

March 2014

SINCE I'VE BEGUN TAKING Gabapentin again I've been questioning the wisdom of my decision to do so. Any benefit Gabapentin may have in reducing negative effects of my illness seems to be outweighed by its soporific effect on me. I feel just as poorly as I ever have, on or off of Gabapentin or Cymbalta, and I've come to refer to Gabapentin capsules as my sleeping pills because I feel the need to sleep so much more frequently than when I wasn't taking Gabapentin. I think the increase in my neuropathic pain and other MS symptoms has perhaps nothing whatever to do with medication I may or may not be taking, but is inevitable on the route of progressive relapsing MS. As my illness has progressed, this is what the tyrant time has left in his wake for me to live with.

Some friends have asked about my MRI at the end of January, but I won't know the outcome until I see my neurologist in mid April. That may also be the time I talk to him about getting off my 'sleeping pills' again.

And so it goes for us all as we're towed along by the tyrant time; often tempted, always taunted, and sometimes even teased or tickled by his tactics. The tyrant does his rarely tender task leaving us to make our choices as best we can. But regardless of what's been left for me in the trickle of its wake, time never can undo me for its torrent comes from God. "He reached from on high, he took me, he drew me out of mighty waters."(2 Sam 22:17)

So I'll wait until April and then perhaps decide to just go with the flow of my progressive illness, stop taking Gabapentin, and hopefully be less groggy. Perhaps in that way I'll be equipped to better wear the pain of progression, and be more aware of his soft strength beneath me, and his life-transforming presence in me And on this first day of spring, when it indeed feels quite wintry still, all the more reason for me to focus on "those 'high mid-summer pomps' in which our Leader, the Son of Man, already dwells, and to which He is calling us."[1] "The miracles that have already happened are, of course, as Scripture so often says, the first fruits of that cosmic summer which is presently coming on."[2]

Savouring spring and eager for Easter,
Colleen

---

1. Lewis, *God in the Dock*, 88.
2. Ibid., 87.

Someone Said a Prayer and Someone Asked Some Questions

April 2014

In *A Diary of Private Prayer*, John Baillie, a Church of Scotland minister wrote, "Thou art hidden behind the curtain of sense, incomprehensible in Thy greatness, mysterious in Thine almighty power; yet here I speak with Thee familiarly as child to parent, as friend to friend. If I could not thus speak to Thee, then were I indeed without hope in the world."[1]

God are you also hidden behind the curtain of senselessness, behind the curtain of my senses gone awry? Are you hidden somewhere, somehow, in the fiery pins and needles that crawl further along and squeeze tighter around my legs and arms, my hands and feet? God are you there hidden behind the curtain of pins and needles swept across my face and rubbed into my eye? Are you hidden in my anemic arms and aching hands, in my heavy head? There are days when I'm weary of hide and seek, times when I'm too worn out from pain to try and find your mercies masquerading as miseries. Can it be? Will there be purpose in my pain if I partner rwith you? And will you help me please if I do?

In his Letters, Samuel Rutherford said, "There is no sweeter fellowship with Christ than to bring our sores and our wounds to Him. There is as much in our Lord's pantry as will satisfy all

---

1. Bailie, *A Diary of Private Prayer*, 41.

his bairns, and as much wine in his cellar as will quench all their thirst."[2] I am expecting some answers I can live with, and am hoping for a vintage to help suffer life's exasperation.

I too have found misery and mercy to be mysteriously matched.

Love,
Colleen

2. Rutherford, *The Letters of Samuel Rutherford*, 8.

Driven or Dragged

June 2014

EARLY IN THE SPRING, after beginning to take Gabapentin again, I began to question my wisdom in doing so because I was sensing a nagging need to sleep, and fatigue is one of the possible side effects of the drug. As it was having minimal to no positive effect on my neuropathy I weaned myself off of Gabapetin completely, hoping to become more alert and less tired in the process, but I noticed I wanted to sleep just as much without Gabapentin in my system as when I was taking it. However, I suspect I yearned for sleep because sleep was my escape from the pain that escalated as I decreased my dosage of Gabapentin. I perceived I'd progressed to a more intense level of pain than what I lived with last summer when I took myself off of Gabapentin for a time. I don't remember any of my pain having ever been as acute as it was when I was without Gabapentin most recently.

After I'm in bed, sleep is long in coming due to pain, but when I'm finally asleep I usually sleep eight hours and don't feel the pain while asleep. So while Gabapentin made me groggy, in a sense 'dragging' me to sleep, the heightened pain resulting from disease progression drove me to sleep because sleep is my escape from pain. Physical pain in and of itself is exhausting, and knowing I'll have a reprieve from it while sleeping urges me to try and sleep more than I used to.

After a time, I opted for being dragged to sleep by drugs rather than driven to sleep by pain, and titrated back on to Gabapentin. I'm hoping that in time the neuropathic pain during my waking hours will be tempered by the maximum dosage of Gabapentin I've recently reached.

The other physical anomaly that has progressed perniciously in recent months is my instability. For ten years now I have lived with the sensation of being on a floating dock, and the risk of falling, not only when running but also while walking or even standing, was most recently realized in February.

While staying in some friends' condo in Mexico, I lost my balance in the bathroom and on my way to the floor cracked my head on the marble vanity. The ER doctor called in a plastic surgeon who used eighteen stitches to close the wound that Len said exposed my skull.

The combined effect of greater instability and persistent pain has been a growing reluctance to participate in group social settings, an effect that reminds me that my illness has sadly altered my demeanor. I much prefer one-on-one interaction with friends and family, no longer keen to attend group events as I once was.

In my last letter, I wrote of my expectation of some answers to the question of whether or not God was present in my pain. It was while reading J.I. Packer's book, Knowing God that I found my answer:

"These things are written for our learning: for the same wisdom which ordered the paths which God's saints trod in Bible times orders the Christian's life today We should not therefore be too taken aback when unexpected and upsetting and discouraging things happen to us now. What do they mean? Why simply that God in his wisdom means to make something of us which we have not attained yet, and is dealing with us accordingly."[1]

Packer goes on to include a list of examples of what God may be trying to teach us, concluding with the suggestion that perhaps God's purpose is simply to draw us into conscious communion with him. "We may be frankly bewildered at things that happen to

1. Packer, Knowing God, 108.

us, but God knows exactly what he is doing, and what he is after, in the handling of our affairs. Always, and in everything, he is wise; we shall see that hereafter, even where we never saw it here. (Job in heaven knows the full reason why he was afflicted, though he never knew it in his life.) Meanwhile we ought not to hesitate to trust his wisdom, even when he leaves us in the dark."[2]

God give us grace in all our own troubles to do so. Thank you for reading once more.

Love,
Colleen

2. Ibid., 109.

Pain, Petulance and Praise

August 2014

"Praise is due to you, O God, in Zion; and to you shall vows be performed, O you who answer prayer! To you all flesh shall come. Praise the LORD! Praise the LORD from the heavens; praise him in the heights above. Praise him, all angels; praise him, all his heavenly hosts. Praise him, sun and moon; praise him, all you shining stars. Praise him, you highest heavens and you waters above the skies. (Ps. 65:1–2, 148:1–4) You praise the heartbreaking beauty of Jessye Norman singing the Vier Letzte Lieder of Richard Strauss. You praise the new puppy for making its offering on the lawn for once, instead of on the living-room rug. Maybe you yourself are praised for some generous thing you have done. In each case, the praise that is handed out is a measured response. It is a matter of saying something to one degree or another complementary, with the implication that if Jessye Norman's voice had sprung a leak or the puppy hadn't made it outside in time or your generous deed turned out to be secretly self-serving, a different sort of response altogether would have been called for.

The way Psalm 148 describes it praising God is another kettle of fish altogether. It is about as measured as a volcanic eruption, and there is no implication that under any conceivable circumstances it could be anything other than what it is. The whole of creation is in on the act—the sun and moon, the sea, fire and snow, Holstein cows and white-throated sparrows, old men in walkers and children who still haven't taken their first step. Their praise is not chiefly a matter of saying anything, because most of creation doesn't deal in words. Instead, the snow whirls, the fire roars, the Holstein bellows, the old man watches the moon rise. Their praise is not something that at their most complimentary they say, but something that at their truest they are.

We learn to praise God not by paying compliments, but by paying attention. Watch how the trees exult when the wind is in them. Mark the utter stillness of the great blue heron in the swamp. Listen to the sound of the rain. Learn how to say, "Hallelujah" from the ones who say it right."[1]

A few weeks ago I had a crash course in learning how to say "Hallelujah" from the ones who say it right. At my behest, Len and I tackled an overnight canoeing/fishing trip, something we'd not done in more than a dozen years.

Although the sensation of burning sandpaper on my palms caused by the canoe paddle shaft rotating in my hands was distressful, carrying loads over the portage's anything but level terrain was my biggest challenge; and my two gentle tumbles made clear to me that I shouldn't try God's patience and ever do it again.

Two weeks later some pain remained, but pain or no pain, praise was plentiful in those idyllic surroundings, praise from nature to the Creator and praise from my heart in response.

My hope is to praise him not only when I feel the short-term self-inflicted pain of a canoe trip, but also when I'm feeling the prolonged and penetrating pain of PRMS. Sometimes it's hard to see the light.

It's more pleasant to pander to pain privately rather than in public, be it to complain about how miserable I am, or be it to touch walls or furniture to gain a sense of stability as I move about, or be it simply to sit, as is increasingly the case.

These ways of indulging pervasive pain and coping with escalating incapacity are easier to do in the privacy of my own home or space, and so I care increasingly less to be out and about in public. Attending several large group events in the last few months

1. Buechner, *Wishful Thinking*, 84–5.

has shown me again that to do so means to pay a price in the days that follow.

Though God permits my pain, he also presides over it. And frightening though my pain is, and the thoughts it can produce are, pain will not keep me. The LORD is my keeper. (Ps 121)

This having been said, I confess to times of feeling swallowed by my vulnerability, prey not only to my pain and incapacities but to my petulance, the by-product of my impatience with God's seeming lackadaisical attitude toward my physical deterioration. "Beneath our clothes, our reputations, our pretensions, beneath our religion or lack of it, we are all vulnerable both to the storm without and to the storm within."[2] But we go over the mountains and under the stars, and life goes on, storms notwithstanding. So too, pray God, may my praise of him go on.

Some reading this update may find my last statement incredible, and to those who do I can only say, that it is knowing how Jesus Christ carries me that permits me to say it.

> "It is as impossible for man to demonstrate the existence of God as it would be for even Sherlock Holmes to demonstrate the existence of Arthur Conan Doyle.
>
> All-wise. All-powerful. All-loving. All-knowing. We bore to death both God and ourselves with our chatter. God cannot be expressed but only experienced.
>
> In the last analysis, you cannot pontificate but only point. A Christian is one who points at Christ and says, "I can't prove a thing, but there's something about his eyes and his voice. There's something about the way he carries his head, his hands. The way he carries his cross. The way he carries me."[3]

I thank God he carries me, along with many others.

Love,
Colleen

---

2. Buechner, *Telling the Truth,* 33.

3. Ibid., *Wishful Thinking,* 36–7.

A Decade or a Day
November 2014

I BRACE MYSELF WHEN I sense that someone is about to touch me, because I know that though the intent of the touch is kind, the sensation of the physical contact will be painful; a sensation akin to hot sandpaper being rubbed across or pressed into my skin or, as someone else described it, acid under their skin. This is one aspect of my relentless neuropathic pain, which has been escalating during the last ten years, and become a painful and presumed constant in my life.

I am sad and vexed to know that the sense of touch is dreadfully distorted in my body. I hate the fact that it's happening, but would hate it much more were it happening to one of our children. I can still hear myself saying to Len, those ten long years ago, having just received a phone call from my doctor asking me to get to emergency as quickly as possible for a cat scan, "Thank God it's not one of the kids." And I remember, too, Len's words, "So now we know it's not cancer, but what's it like to live with MS?" spoken to me ten long weeks later when I told him the news I'd just received that the lesions in my brain were not malignant but appeared to indicate I had multiple sclerosis.

At the time, I was so overcome with relief at not having a brain tumour that MS didn't seem to warrant a second thought. I knew MS was a prevalent illness in Manitoba and thought if many people lived with it, surely there'd be plenty of assistance and information to help me cope with this disease.

But two and a half years later I began to discover there was a vast arena of unknown I would live in, and that the unknown is territory where fear can fester. I now fear the fact that longevity is in my genes.

If, in one decade my disease has progressed to the point where at fifty-five I'm asked by someone on virtually every run I take whether I need help, will I even be able to run in another ten years from now?

Run . . . Who am I kidding, run? I call it running because I began running thirty-six years ago and only this year has my running begun to alarm strangers who see me on the road; kind strangers who stop and sometimes even turn around and come back to ask me if I'm okay. They may be strangers to me but clearly they are not strangers to God. They are those who've noticed my gimp and have obeyed God's nudge to ask me if I need help.

The same route that took me thirty minutes to run six years ago, now takes me forty minutes to complete as I shuffle along hoping with each stride that I'll lift my legs high enough to avoid another abrupt and painful meeting with the road.

But, never mind will I be able to run ten years from now, I fear I may not even be walking five years from now. Many of my ancestors died in their nineties, and the thought of a possible thirty years in a wheelchair scares me.

But a fear that looms larger than the fear of an imminent wheelchair is the fear that my irritability (chronic pain's persistent partner) will drive from me those I hold closest to my heart.

With each passing day I feel more poorly. I sense my irritability and unkindness following the same curve as my pain and I wonder how much irascibility I can expect those I live with to tolerate before walls go up to shield themselves from the peevish woman I've become. Self-pity is ugly, I know.

Please God, it's not too late to mend my ways, and to wear on my sleeve John Baillie's prayer "Let me use pains as material for endurance."[1]

---

1. Baillie, *A Diary of Private Prayer*, 101.

The floating dock I feel like I've been on since November 2004 is riding increasingly rough waters, making me totter, raising my risk of falling, and compelling me to use banisters, railings, walls and people for the stability I need to avert tumbles and collisions.

Not every decennial is marked with pleasure.

What manifested itself in November 2004 as a mild tingling sensation in the tip of my left pinkie, has insidiously enveloped my body, head and face over the last ten years, the mild tingling escalating to the point where my left arm and hand have been rendered virtually useless from pain and weakness, while neck, shoulder, leg and head pain persist during my waking hours.

Much of my body has succumbed to sporadic tonic spasms and constant dysaesthesia that intensifies with any touch or pressure including shoes, clothing and bed linens. Occasionally I'll wake with sharp cramps in my legs that exacerbate my limp and pain the next day. The pressure required to grip a pot handle or a jug of milk, or to hold a book, or to hold anything for that matter, creates a burning, aching sensation in my left palm, wrist and arm, while the weight-bearing required to stand, walk or run induces the same sort of pain in my left foot, ankle and leg.

A decade or a day, the pain won't go away.

With every passing day, it seems it's here to stay.

I run and walk with pain because life isn't static and I simply can't not walk and run. So I've resolved to limp and gimp with my pain until I'm no longer able to because I don't see not walking and running as an option, and I'm banking on God to be with me each stumbling step of the way.

> For you, O Lord, are my hope,
> my trust, O Lord, from my youth.
> Upon you I have leaned from my birth;
> it was you who took me from my mother's womb.
> My praise is continually of you. (Ps 71: 5–6)

A decade after the initial fear-filled symptoms appeared, I've come to know that I live not only in an arena fraught with fear, but also in a larger arena filled with freedom, where the unknown is tethered to time. And though time is a tyrant, it's also a teacher, tenderly transforming me ever on target and leading me home.

The years of not knowing what would come became, with time, years of knowing something will. This is not all there is. There is more to come; freedom from illness, freedom from pain, freedom from fears and from unfulfilled dreams.

How this freedom will play out of course only time can tell. It remains as much a mystery to me as I myself am a mystery to me.

Knowing the Master of all mysteries will preside, I will do no other but wince through my present pain, and ponder the beauty in clouds and wherever else I might find it.

I will strive to let nothing of value be lost on me, and pine for the beauty that is promised to come when all things will be new.

"And the one who was seated on the throne said, 'See, I am making all things new.'" (Rev 21:5)

I remain grateful for hope, for promises, and for prayers.

Love,
Colleen

Panorama

March 2015

I WAS GROWING TIRED of writing updates exclusively about me, and was pleasantly surprised when this early morning's pink sky prompted me to begin this time with some recent images of the Peters panorama.

A couple of weeks ago, Jackson purchased a ticket to Athens, because in six weeks he'll be sailing on the Aegean aboard The Encounter; a 90 ft gaff rigged schooner, beginning a seven week impact training program with Torchbearers International, a global community of believers in the saving and transforming life of Jesus Christ.

More recently, Nicholas applied for a ten week Adventure Bible School program beginning in just under a year with the Torchbearers on New Zealand's north island. Several weeks ago, Renée purchased a ticket to Australia, to take advantage of the opportunity she's been given by friends to do a graphic design mentorship in Melbourne this summer. Victoria, on the other hand, is content to stay put in Victoria for now, this being quite evident when Len, the boys and I spent the first week of February enjoying a reprieve from our Winnipeg winter visiting Victoria at her very appealing home turf on Vancouver Island.

In a bittersweet sort of way, our children grow up so very quickly don't they? Although Len and I too are staying put for now, we've finally bought a stationary bike so now on the minus forty degree days I can work up a sweat without running outside to do so.

I recently saw a powerful movie that haunts me still, about a fifty-year old woman living with early onset alzheimer's. In a poignant address given to an alzheimer support group at Columbia university, Alice speaks about learning to master the art of losing, and about the many and varied ways she and her family have experienced and will continue to experience losses. Though progressive losses are something I can relate to, her words moved me deeply, honed my perspective, and brought to mind a thought I spoke to Len on the way home from the cinema, "I'd so much rather slowly lose my body than my mind."

I've also read a book recently, *The Enduring Melody*, written by Michael Mayne, an Anglican priest and writer. In this very personal journal written during the last year of his losing battle with jaw cancer, Mayne reflects on time and eternity, and writes words that struck me as profoundly true:

> John Taylor in *The Go-Between God*, presents us with a striking image; Do we see ourselves, set in the living stream of history and the moment that is now, as facing the downstream flow, so that our 'now' is coming from behind us and carrying with it all the debris from the past? If so, we are imprisoned in the contradiction between what is and what might have been. Or do we picture ourselves facing upstream, so that our 'now' is always coming to meet us, for then our task is to rise to the challenge of what is and what might be. The first way, however realistic, contains nothing of hope or expectation.[1]

It was a timely read for me as days and nights of prevailing pain and increasing disability drag on, an irrational guilt in their wide wake. When spirits ebb it's good to be reminded of a more promising way to live my life, a way I pray that those I hold close to my heart will live theirs.

Love,
Colleen

1. Mayne, *The Enduring Melody*, 197.

Epilogue

As a youngster, one of our children, whenever ill, railed against Adam and Eve for having brought evil and sickness into the world through their disobedience to God in the garden. In the days before Easter this year, I grasped in a way new to me, the justice of God's punishment for that disobedience, the scope of suffering which that punishment wrought on the creation God loves, and the fact that since then nothing on earth has been as God meant it to be. I understood with fresh clarity that prior to the justice God will bring at the culmination of history, evil can afflict randomly and often in seemingly unjust ways beyond my comprehension. God is sovereign yet still surrendered himself to suffer that my sins could be wiped clean away. My suffering, though not understandable, is meaningful and can be trusted to the God who suffered for me—suffers with me—and who, through suffering will conquer evil and ultimately make all things new.

These ideas help me cope with both my most familiar MS miseries that continue with increasing intensity, and with newer neuropathic pains as they arrive. I've been reminded recently too, that because God is sovereign these nasty neuropathic anomalies in my life will work out for good; that the clean slate God has given me can't be taken from me, and that the best is yet to come. Between now and then I pray I'll have eyes to see God's good graces undergirding me as I go, and a grateful heart that yearns to tell of it.

Writing letters over the years has been a cathartic endeavour for me—both the telling and the hearing of my story playing a crucial role in my journey toward wholeness.

God met me in wonderful ways at the critical outset of my illness and the magnitude of his presence has not waned as time has passed and I've struggled with the effects of an incurable progressive disease. The reality of God's presence permeating my days is the impetus for this book, and writing about it has given me profound pleasure.

Bibliography

Augustine. *The Confessions*. Peabody: Hendrickson, 2004

Baillie, John. *A Diary of Private Prayer*. New York: Simon and Schuster, 2014.

Benson, Herbert. *Timeless Healing: The Power and Biology of Belief*. New York: Simon and Schuster, 1997.

Berry, Wendell. *Sabbaths*. San Francisco: North Point, 1987.

Boyd, Jeffrey H. *Being Sick Well*. Ada: Baker, 2005.

Brown, Gerald M, trans. *The Abbreviated Psalter of the Venerable Bede*. Grand Rapids: Eerdmans, 2002.

Buechner, Frederick. *Wishful Thinking: A Seeker's ABC*. New York: Harper Collins, 1973.

———. *A Room Called Remember: Uncollected Pieces*. New York: HarperCollins, 1992.

———. *The Faces of Jesus: A Life Story*. Brewster: Paraclete, 2014.

———. *Secrets in the Dark: A Life in Sermons*. New York: HarperCollins, 2006.

———. *Telling the Truth: The Gospel as Tragedy, Comedy, and Fairy Tale*. New York: HarperCollins, 1977.

Cameron, William B. *Informal Sociology: A Casual Introduction to Sociological Thinking*. New York: Random House, 1963.

Carcione, Joseph. Reviewer. "Pain and Multiple Sclerosis." WebMD. Published November 2, 2006. http://www.webmd.com/multiple-sclerosis/features/pain-multiple-sclerosis.

Chesterton, Gilbert K. *Orthodoxy*. Peabody: Hendrickson, 2006.

Connor, George, ed. *Listening to Your Life: Daily Meditations with Frederick Buechner*. New York: HarperCollins, 1992.

Farjeon, Eleanor. "Morning Has Broken, Like the First Morning." In *Common Praise*, Toronto: Anglican Book Centre, 1998.

Foster, Richard J. *Prayer: Finding the Heart's True Home*. New York: HarperCollins, 1992.

———. *Celebration of Discipline*. New York: HarperCollins, 2007.

Foster, Richard J., and James Bryan Smith, eds. *Devotional Classics: Selected Readings for Individuals and Groups*. New York: HarperCollins, 1993.

Hays, Edward. *In Pursuit of the Great White Rabbit.* Quoted in Job, Rueben P. and

Norman Shawchuk. *A Guide to Prayer for All Who Seek God.* Nashville: The Upper Room, 1983.

Heschel, unkown source, quoted in "Now that I am Old I Admire Kind People. Rabbie Abraham Joshua Heschel." http://www.jewishjournal. com/rabbijohnrosovesblog/item/now_that_i_am_old_i_admire_kind_ people._rabbi_abraham_joshua_heschel, line 13.

Job, Rueben P. and Norman Shawchuk. *A Guide to Prayer for All God's People.* Nashville: The Upper Room, 1990.

———. *A Guide to Prayer for All Who Seek God.* Nashville: The Upper Room, 2003.

———. *A Guide to Prayer for Ministers and Other Servants.* Nashville: The Upper Room, 1983.

John of the Cross. "Sayings of Light and Love" *in The Collected Works of St John of the Cross.* Translated by Kieran Kavanaugh and Otilio Rodriguez. Washington: ICS Publications, 1991.

Julian of Norwich. *Showings.* New York: Paulist, 1978.

Kreeft, "The Problem of Good and Evil," *YouTube* video, 15:40. May 27, 2104. https://www.youtube.com/watch?v=W2NmwGGoXPE

Lewis, C.S. *God in the Dock: Essays on Theology and Ethics.* Edited by Walter Hooper. Grand Rapids: Erdmans, 1970.

———. *The Beloved Works of C.S. Lewis.* New York: Inspirational, 1998.

———. *The Problem of Pain.* New York: HarperCollins, 1940.

———. *The Weight of Glory and Other Addresses.* New York: HarperOne, 2001.

———. *The Wisdom of Lewis.* Compiled by Brian Sibley. Louisville: Westminster John Knox, 1997.

Manning, Martha. *Chasing Grace: Reflections of a Catholic Girl, Grown Up.* New York: HarperCollins, 1996.Mayne, Michael. *The Enduring Melody.* London: Dartman,

Longman and Todd, 2006. MS Answers. "What is Progressive MS?" http:// www.msanswers.ca/ContentPage.aspx?L=2&page=progressive1

Nouwen, Henri. *The Wounded Healer: Ministry in Contemporary Society.* New York: Image, 1979.

———. *With Open Hands.* Toronto: Ave Maria, 1972.

Oliver, Mary. *Evidence: Poems by Mary Oliver.* Boston: Beacon, 2009.

Packer, James I. *Knowing God.* London: Hodder and Stoughton, 2013.

Parker, Ol and Deborah Moggach, *The Best Marigold Hotel,* DVD, directed by John Madden. Los Angeles, CA:Fox Searchlight Pictures, 2012.

Peterson, Eugene. *The Message.* Colorado Springs: Nav, 1993.

Piper, John. *The Misery of Job and The Mercy of God.* Wheaton: Crossway, 2002.

Rutherford, Samuel. *The Loveliness of Christ: From the Letters of Samuel Rutherford,* edited by Ellen Lister. Reprint, Moscow, ID: Community Christian Ministries, 2012.

Sine, Christine. *Sacred Rhythms: Finding a Peaceful Pace in a Hectic World.* Grand Rapids: Baker, 2003.

Shakespeare, William. *Twelfth Night. Hamlet.* Edited by Bertrand Evans. Macmillan Co.. New York: Collier-Macmillan, 1963.

Stump, Eleanor, "Faith and the Problem of Evil," The Veritas Forum video, XX, February 23, 2002. http://veritas.org/talks/faith-and-the-problem-evil/?view=presenters&speakers_id=2076.

Stuntz, William J., "Three Gifts for Hard Times," *Christianity Today.* August 2009.

Swenson, Kristen. *Living Through Pain: Psalms and the Search for Wholeness.* Waco: Baylor University Press, 2005.

Taylor, Barbara B. *An Altar in The World.* New York: HarperCollins, 2009.

Tennyson, Lord Alfred. *Idylls of the King.*1859; Project Gutenberg, 2008. http://www.gutenberg.org/ebooks/610

The Lord of the Rings: Fellowship of the Ring. Directed by Peter Jackson. 2001. Burbank, CA: Warner Home Video, 2011. DVD.

Thompson, Alan. "Primary Progressive Multiple Sclerosis," *MS Matters 39.* London: MS Society, 2001.

Tolkien, John R.R. *The Lord of the Rings: Fellowship of the Ring.* London: HarperCollins, 2011.

Volf, Miroslav. *Free of Charge:Giving and Forgiving in a Culture of Stripped of Grace.* Grand Rapids: Zondervan, 2006.

Wells, Samuel. *Be Not Afraid: Facing Fear with Faith.* Grand Rapids: Brazos, 2011.

Willard, Dallas. *The Divine Conspiracy: Rediscovering Our Hidden Life in God.* HarperCollins, 2009.

Yancey, Philip. *When We Hurt:Prayer, Preparation, and Hope for Life's Pain.* Grand Rapids: Zondervan, 2006.

Yancey, Philip and Paul Brand. *The Gift of Pain: Why We Hurt and What We Can Do about It.* Grand Rapids: Zondervan, 1997.